the art & craft of writing

CHRISTIAN FICTION

the art & craft of writing

CHRISTIAN FICTION

THE COMPLETE GUIDE TO FINDING YOUR STORY, HONING YOUR SKILLS, & GLORIFYING GOD IN YOUR NOVEL

WritersDigest.*com*
Cincinnati, Ohio

Jeff Gerke

 Published by Writer's Digest Books, an imprint of F+W Media, Inc., 10151 Carver Road, Suite # 200, Blue Ash, OH 45242. (800) 289-0963. First edition.

For more resources for writers, visit www.writersdigest.com.

18 17 16 15 14 5 4 3 2 1

Distributed in Canada by Fraser Direct
100 Armstrong Avenue
Georgetown, Ontario, Canada L7G 5S4
Tel: (905) 877-4411

Distributed in the U.K. and Europe by F&W Media International
Brunel House, Newton Abbot, Devon, TQ12 4PU, England
Tel: (+44) 1626-323200, Fax: (+44) 1626-323319
E-mail: postmaster@davidandcharles.co.uk

Distributed in Australia by Capricorn Link
P.O. Box 704, Windsor, NSW 2756 Australia
Tel: (02) 4577-3555

ISBN 13 9781599638744

Edited by Cris Freese
Interior designed by Bethany Rainbolt
Cover designed by Aly Yorio
Production coordinated by Debbie Thomas

DEDICATION

To my precious daughter
Sophia Song Taylor Gerke
God moved heaven and earth to bring us to you, Sophie
And you to us

TABLE OF CONTENTS

FOREWORD

By Jerry B. Jenkins

What eager, hopeful writer is a scared, uncertain beginner, unpublished and unknown?

A. You
B. Me
C. Stephen King
D. John Grisham
E. Karen Kingsbury
F. Francine Rivers
G. All of the above

Drum roll. The answer is G.

Surprised?

The trick is when the question is asked. Regardless of what "name" novelist you can think of, all were once where you are now.

There was nothing wrong with being a wannabe, but I tended to forget that those who had what I wanted, those doing what I longed to do, were once invisible, too. I assumed that the novelists I looked up to—the Marjorie Holmses, the John D. MacDonalds, the Robert Ludlums—had somehow been birthed full grown in their agents' New York offices.

The fact is they all had to learn the craft, hone their skills, pay their dues.

You want to be a Christian novelist? You came to the right book. Jeff Gerke can guide you there, provided you recognize that fiction writing is no game, no hobby, no diversion for dilettantes.

If you learn nothing else from these pages, I hope they'll unveil to you that writing is work. What flows easy from your keyboard today reads hard tomorrow. Real writing is rewriting. Whatever creativity you bring to the task must be tempered by true humility and an awareness of the poverty of your ability.

With the explosion of publishing opportunities these days, the competition for readers is greater than ever. But the fact that it's easier than ever to expose your writing to the public—on websites, in blogs, via independent and traditional publishing—doesn't change the fact that cream still rises to the top. You need to be the one rising, because you're reading a book like this.

Don't apologize for wanting your writing to stand out. Your motive for wanting to be a novelist should be that you have something to say. As a Christian you have a message. You've been told you have a way with words, a knack for this. If you're holding a hard copy of this book, nestle the spine in your palm and fan the pages with your thumb slowly enough to get a picture of the scope of the topics you'll want to master. If you're reading it electronically, cursor through.

Does that convince you this is more than a hobby?

How badly do you want it? You can breeze through this book in a few hours and pretend to be an insider. Or you can make this the bible of your craft for a season and let Jeff Gerke serve as your mentor as you launch your journey toward becoming a Christian novelist.

I'm living the dream as a full-time Christian novelist, writing what I believe in and care about. The path is crowded and the passage long, but the rewards are eternal. Consider this book your ticket.

Now fasten your seatbelt.

Jerry B. Jenkins, author of more than 180 books with sales of more than seventy million copies, including the best-selling Left Behind series, owns the Christian Writers Guild. Twenty of his books have reached *The New York Times* bestseller list (seven debuting at number one). *I, Saul* (Worthy Publishing), Jenkins's most recent book, has been described as *The DaVinci Code* meets *The Robe*, combining a modern-day thriller with a historical novel.

PREFACE

This book arose out of a series of tips I wrote for a website during 2006 and 2007. In those days, I was convinced that I had figured out the best way to write fiction and that everyone should do it this way or risk being just wrong.

I have since mellowed.

I now understand that very few things can be considered true "laws" or "rules" of fiction. Indeed, I now believe in only one, which I call the Great Commandment of Fiction: You must engage your reader from beginning to end. Everything else is just preference, opinion, and style.

But I hadn't realized that back in 2006.

In preparation for the release of this version of *The Art & Craft of Writing Christian Fiction*, I went through the manuscript again trying to soften the "my way or the highway" tone, but you can still sense it occasionally.

In those spots, please forgive my youthful conviction/intolerance and instead receive it all as a set of suggestions coming from one writer's preferences and style. If you prefer to write another way, or if you disagree on one or several points, that's fine. Allow the more mature me to apologize for the more certain me, and to give you permission to use the instruction here that resonates with you and to ditch the rest.

You might try a few of these techniques, even if you feel you don't agree, just to see if you do like them. Sort of like an oil painter taking a pottery class just to check it out. You might find your new passion or a technique or two that significantly helps you in your own fiction. But if you don't, that's okay, too!

Enjoy.

—Jeff Gerke

INTRODUCTION

I love Christian fiction.

I love writing it. I love editing it. I love teaching it at writers' conferences. And I love publishing it through my small publishing house, Marcher Lord Press.

Moreover, I love the people who write Christian fiction. Christian novelists are among my dearest friends. Where else can you find such imagination, playfulness, and depth of thought? Who else but a novelist can you ask how to murder someone and dispose of the body—and not have them call the police on you? Who else would go to a famous landmark and compete with you to find the best spot for the villain to make his nefarious escape?

Let's face it: Christian fiction is fun. Even if you're writing a serious-minded study of man's inhumanity to man, there is something exhilarating about story, about creating people and worlds and events, about telling a tale that keeps readers enraptured and maybe—just maybe—leaves them fortified in their walk with Jesus.

But for all the fun, it's also hard work. There is skill involved in writing excellent Christian fiction. There is craftsmanship to be learned. And there are the long hours pounding away on a manuscript that, by the time you're done with it, has you convinced it's the worst piece of garbage ever penned by man.

That's not even talking about trying to get your book published. It's a wonder anyone would choose such a way to spend otherwise useful time.

So maybe you put your novel away for a while. You've tried to do more sensible things with your spare moments. You've attempted to be engaged with workaday matters, laundry, and bills.

But one day, a new story idea will pop into your head, or you won't be able to stop hearing the voice of a character demanding to be written about. On that day, you'll be right back where you were, counting the cost of writing Christian fiction—and loving it like nothing else.

ABOUT ME

I officially began my love affair with Christian fiction back in 1994 when I got my first publishing contracts (with Multnomah Publishers). Unofficially, it was the moment I became a Christian and tried to imagine what it would've been like to walk beside Jesus on the shores of the Sea of Galilee. And before that, I'd had a love of story that stretched back to my days of playing with my G.I. Joe action figures.

I published three novels in the late '90s—near-future techno-thrillers that were, ahem, ahead of their time. Then I took the first of several jobs on the editorial staff of a Christian publishing company, also with Multnomah. In total I've had six novels published (so far); worked for three publishing companies (so far); and performed edits, critiques, and brainstorming sessions on thousands of Christian novels.

I have worked on all sides of the publishing process. I've been author, editor, and publisher. I've been the low guy on the totem pole, and I've run fiction departments. I've been junior flunky, and I've been publisher. I've worked for others, and I've worked for myself. I've taught Christian fiction at writers' conferences around the United States.

WHAT IS THIS BOOK?

Through it all, I've developed my own school of thought regarding the way Christian fiction should be written. My body of experience has resulted in a vast collection of best practices, things to avoid, and important guidelines. For two years I wrote these thoughts out and presented them to the public through my "Fiction Writing Tip of the Week" column at one of my sites: www.WhereTheMapEnds.com.

After ninety-six weekly tips, I started realizing something: I'd said it all. Just about everything I saw in any manuscript I edited, I'd already commented on in the column.

It was great. I was able to refer people to the site instead of typing it up all over again. If they needed help introducing major characters, I could send them to Tip 15. If they needed to learn the principles of good dialogue, they could read Tips 46–49. Whether it was matters of character, time bombs, or dumb puppets, it was all there on the column.

I should mention that, as I've mellowed with age, I've become less strident about what is "right" or "wrong" about writing fiction. My later fiction craft books with Writer's Digest reflect this more easy-going approach.

I began to wonder what I could do next. I didn't have new tips to write every week, because I had pretty much said it all. Yet, I wanted to keep teaching. Then the e-mails came in: "This should be in a book. I'd buy this thing in a heartbeat. I don't always like reading off the screen."

Eureka!

The Art & Craft of Writing Christian Fiction is my "Fiction Writing Tip of the Week" column in book form. Plus, there are a few extra tips you won't find anywhere else. The tips are arranged thematically and have been edited for this medium, but you're holding in your hands the entire Jeff Gerke school of writing Christian fiction.

A CONVENIENT ARRANGEMENT

As I surveyed my Tips, I realized they fell into major groupings. There were several Tips about writing a novel but also several about selling a book, editing a book, or even strategizing it. There were Tips about how to think about yourself as a novelist and how to think of God in the process. These groupings suggested the organization of *The Art & Craft of Writing Christian Fiction*.

Part I covers the spiritual aspects of writing Christian fiction. These chapters help you make sure your head is in the right place when you sit down to write.

Part II covers strategic matters as you think about your book: things like creating your characters and establishing the mechanisms that cause suspense. This part contains the first of five sections titled "Focus on the Craft." These sections are multiple chapters grouped around a common topic. They're similar to intensive workshops, right here in this book.

Part III, the largest section of the book, covers actually writing your novel. We look at showing versus telling, description, dialogue, point of view, and everything else you need to keep in mind as you're writing. This section contains the other four "Focus on the Craft" sections in the book.

Between these pages you will find everything about the art and craft of actually writing Christian fiction. And hopefully, while you're learning, worshipping, and revising feverishly, you'll get a few grins along the way.

LET'S GET ARTSY AND CRAFTY, SHALL WE?

I love Christian fiction. About the only thing I love more than writing it is encouraging others to write it. I cherish the remarks I've received from conference attendees and editing clients who tell me that my input has helped them better achieve what they were hoping to accomplish with their novel. I want to serve God by equipping Christian novelists to go out and tell that portion of the Good News that He has given them to write through fiction.

So pour yourself a cup of your favorite drink and cozy up in your reading spot. It's time to get serious about the fun that is the art and craft of writing Christian fiction.

PART I

THE SPIRITUAL HEART OF WRITING CHRISTIAN FICTION

chapter 1

AN (ACCEPTING) AUDIENCE OF ONE

I want to start out this book by giving you the best tip of all: Be sure you understand Who you're writing for and why you're writing it for Him.

As a Christian novelist, you may be writing fiction for any number of reasons. Maybe you just love to tell stories. Maybe you can't help yourself. Maybe you want to spread the creativity you've been given. Maybe you want to use gifts God has given you. You may even want to use fiction to get messages across to as wide an audience as possible.

These are wonderful motivations, but they're not the whole picture.

There are less savory motives, too. Some writers turn to fiction because someone told them they would never amount to anything, and they want to prove the naysayer wrong. They may be writing to create a world that serves their every base desire. They may be trying to show off, look important, or leave their mark on the world.

I can tell you from experience that none of those motives is where the action is really at.

I spent a lot of years thinking I wasn't actually worth the air I breathed. I thought writing a novel would make me special or worthwhile. Then I thought that becoming a best-selling author was what I needed. Sadly, even after six novels published, that never happened.

All this made me crazy. I considered doing some dumb things to try to gain more readers and improve my supposed importance.

Only in 2006 did I learn what a joke all that was. I'd given lip service to the idea of writing for an audience of One, but until then I didn't really mean it. It's what I said to console myself because I wasn't getting the success I really wanted.

Finally, God granted me an epiphany. I went through something that was extremely painful, but it resulted in a lesson I wouldn't trade for anything. The epiphany came as I read *Search for Significance* by Robert McGee.

That book told me that my lifelong addiction to approval and seeking validation of others was nothing but false thinking. The truth, McGee wrote, was that God has permanently given me His approval, favor, and delight.

McGee has four categories of ways that Christians often behave if they don't truly believe in God's approval. Such a Christian might become an approval addict, a perfectionist, someone who plays the blame game (because of what it might mean about him if he was actually to blame for something), or someone who feels he is permanently damaged and can never, ever change for the better. If any of those sounds like you, then I plead with you to get McGee's book.

Through it, Jesus Christ freed me to finally begin writing—and living—simply for Him. I am no longer enslaved to achievement or approval. I have all the approval I can ever handle, and it is reserved for me, imperishable and safe, in God's hands.

As long as you write for any other purpose than to glorify God, you will not be writing for the right reasons. You will not be fulfilled. You must get this right from the outset.

Incidentally, wanting to glorify God above all else means you also have to be willing to give up anything—even writing—if He shows you that doing something else would glorify Him more. Anything we are unwilling to let go of is an idol.

chapter 2
EXAMINE YOUR DESIRE TO BE PUBLISHED

Why do you want to be published?

It might be a dream of yours, but what's behind that dream? Is it a need to prove something? A desire to *be* someone? A need to leave your mark on the world? A desire to be rich and/or famous? Do you feel that being published would justify your existence, as I once thought?

If so, I'd like to urge you to reexamine those reasons.

Don't get me wrong: It's not necessarily bad to want to be published. There are dozens of good reasons to want this. But as I've worked with thousands of aspiring novelists over the years, I've encountered quite a few not-so-good reasons, too. I've struggled with some of them myself.

I like to meditate on the idea of contentment. It seems to me that contentment is pretty much the secret to a successful Christian life. I also believe that discontentment is behind just about every sin in our lives.

From the time of Eve to today, most sin begins with this thought: *Wait a minute, I don't have what I deserve.* This leads to an inevitable reaction: *I'm going to grab for myself a bit of what I should've been given in the first place.*

Discontentment leads to greed, which I believe is the inescapable result of thinking we haven't been given what we deserve (or of thinking we have been made to endure something we don't deserve), no matter the category. Don't think of this just in the narrow sense, either—wanting more money or possessions.

When we feel we haven't been given enough of something, we act greedy about that thing. If we believe we have been slighted or gypped, we try to snag some measure of what we feel we've been denied. This could be possessions, sexual gratification, maybe food, or the approval of a certain person or group.

Or maybe it's an insatiable need to be published.

Jesus said to be on our guard against *every form of greed* (Luke 12:15). As a Christian writer, you need to examine your motives for wanting to be published. Do you want it so desperately because you feel it will make you content? Can you be content with your life if you never get published? Or will you not be "happy" until you achieve this goal?

Let me tell you: Being published is nice, but it won't make you content.

Easy for him to say, right? If that's what you're thinking, I understand. But it's still true.

Being published brings its own set of pressures and problems. (For most folks, the main effect of "fame" is that suddenly they have lots of other people wanting the "famous" ones to help them get famous, too.) Being published is a nice feeling, but so is having a chocolate bar. Neither one will align the planets of your solar system or bring you ultimate peace.

If you believe that getting published will finally make all your dreams come true, you believe a lie. And you may be acting out of greed.

No wonder Paul says that greed amounts to idolatry (Colossians 3:5). If you're looking to a publishing contract to make you content, then you're looking to a piece of paper to do something only God can do. If you're looking to something besides God to do something only God can do, that's called idolatry.

So I ask you again: Why do you want to be published? What do you think will come to you if and when that day finally comes?

A PLACE OF FULLNESS

I believe every Christian struggles with areas of greed—areas in which he believes his life would be complete, if only … X.

What's X for you? Marriage? Children? A new car? A new home? A multibook publishing contract?

Again, it's not necessarily wrong to want to change your situation. If you or your loved ones are being abused, it's not wrong to want that to end. If you're living in a dangerous place, and you wish you could get out, it's not wrong to work toward that goal or want that change.

And it's not wrong to want to be published either. If your desire is correct, then I think God loves to grant us the desires of our hearts. Remember, He placed those desires there in the first place!

I launched my own publishing company, Marcher Lord Press, because I was personally "discontented" with the state of Christian publishing, particularly regarding Christian speculative fiction. Through this company, I strive to change the situation.

The question is one of expectations and motives. Did I believe Marcher Lord Press would solve all my problems and bring me inner harmony? No. Even if MLP were to become a massive publishing giant, it wouldn't bring me inner peace.

I have to go through my life with the conviction that *God has given me everything I need for contentment.* I have to believe I'm operating from a place of fullness, not a place of emptiness.

When God used Nathan to rebuke King David, God said He had given David many amazing gifts, "and if that had been too little, I would have added to you many more things like these!"

So it is with us. Our Lord has lavished upon us the riches of His grace and has blessed us with every spiritual blessing. He has given us a life so abundant our cup runs over. We have a life characterized by joy, love, comfort, and the peace of God.

We are, like Adam and Eve, complete in the Garden. As Christians we are equipped with springs of living water welling up to eternal life. We have the powerful, loving, guiding Spirit of God.

What more do we need? What else does God need to add for us to be content?

God is not the great Withholder. He's not the great Gypper. He is the great Giver, the Lavisher, the Father delighted to give us the Kingdom.

COUNTING THOSE CRAZY BLESSINGS

Perhaps it's time for you to do some meditating of your own. Ask God to change your perspective from looking at what you feel you lack to gratefully remembering all he's given you. He hasn't ripped you off.

Remember Paul in Ephesians 3:19. Say with him: I am "filled with the fullness of God" in this area. Say that you have no need to grasp for more or get ahead of the next person; you will no longer believe that true fulfillment will come from even great success in this area.

Even if you're talking about being published.

Maybe you need to surrender your desire to be published. You might need to confess that it's an area where you think God's ripped you off, and you're only acting out of greed to get back what you believe you should've had in the first place. A search for contentment in something beside what God's *already* given is, in fact, idolatry.

Contentment is found only in Jesus Christ—whether you ever get published or not.

chapter 3
THE INVISIBLE NOVELIST

There are a couple of philosophies of writing fiction. One is what I call the painted-paragraphs approach. This is the style of writing fiction in which the author works very hard to make her prose beautiful, textured, poetic, and sensuous. The goal is for the reader to delight in the magnificence of the writer's artistry. It is the words, vocabulary, and deft phrases—the hand of the author herself—that is to be the focus of such a novel.

Another philosophy of fiction is what I call the invisible-novelist approach. In this, the novelist seeks to disappear from his fiction, thus allowing the story and the characters, not the author's own hand, to be what the reader notices.

In my early days, I felt that one of these was *better* than the other. I'm no longer willing to say that, as both are legitimate approaches that can result in fiction that powerfully moves the reader. My personal preference for my own fiction is still the invisible-novelist approach, but if you prefer to paint your paragraphs or approach fiction from yet another direction, I hereby give you license to do so!

WHAT'S AN INVISIBLE NOVELIST?

What does this phrase even mean? How can the novel be written without the novelist?

I don't mean the world should have fewer novelists, but rather that the author should seek to immerse readers so deeply in the story that they forget they're reading a book. In this philosophy, readers should feel the story is *happening to them.*

In other words, the invisible-novelist storyteller should remove himself from the story.

This is sometimes (but certainly not always) a spiritual issue. The author may desire to win the reader's respect or admiration, so he works to keep the spotlight on himself. The novel might be a four-hundred-page way of saying, "Look at me!"

As an author, you want your reader to suspend her disbelief, don't you? Especially in speculative genres, we want to be given license to tell however wild or wacky a tale we want, and we want the reader to stay with us. If this is a goal, then one suggestion would be to stop reminding her that she's reading a book.

Imagine you're trying to watch a DVD at home. You're curled up on the couch with popcorn, the lights dimmed. You slide the DVD in, and the movie begins. Then suddenly the director jumps between you and the TV. "Okay, you're going to love this movie," he says. "My original inspiration for it was something that happened in real life. Oh, my, but mine is an interesting life story. It all began with my mother, so to understand me you need to know my mother's life story. …"

All the while you're craning your neck trying to look past him to see what's happening in the movie.

Finally you get him to sit down, and you begin to get into the movie. In fact, you feel tears welling up in your eyes. Up jumps the director again. "That's going to make you cry, isn't it? I knew it! I have found, in my vast experience as a well-read and well-traveled individual that people can be made to feel emotion if I manipulate the …"

Where did those tears go? Dried up fast. It broke the mood.

Later you're into the movie again, and you're carried away by the special effects in the film. You feel like you're actually soaring through Earth's atmosphere on the way to Mars. You're getting a feeling for what it must be like to be an astron—

"That's all done in the computer; did you know that? I interviewed, like, ten special-effects houses before I finally decided on this one. I didn't like the takeoff here as much as later when they're approaching …"

You get the point. If you're not a fan of the painted-paragraphs philosophy (and many people are), then when the author jumps up and draws attention to himself, you may feel he is breaking the illusion that the reader is truly experiencing the story, and he may be frustrating or irritating the reader.

THE MAGICIAN WHO MADE HIMSELF DISAPPEAR

There are many ways authors can intrude on their story with just as many motives.

As we've seen, some writers do it intentionally because that's the philosophy of fiction they prefer, and that's completely fine. Some writers may simply not realize they're doing it. A dump truck full of backstory, explanation, and exposition may seem to stop the story cold, drawing attention to the fact that the reader is reading a book. Why did the author do this? Sometimes because of inexperience.

Other times the author might interfere because he subconsciously wants to draw attention to himself. Ornate language, "impressive" vocabulary, and the strikingly beautiful turn of phrase are sometimes the results. These things can be okay if they're done simply, because that's the sort of fiction the writer prefers. But sometimes these may be a sign that the author is spiritually out of balance.

No matter what philosophy of fiction you ascribe to, don't try to impress the reader. Don't try to make her think you're an amazing writer unlike any the world has ever seen. The reader probably didn't come to this book to be impressed by a writer. The reader came to be entertained by a story. You want her to love the story, not the storyteller. Be like John the Baptist: Let the story increase while you decrease. Go back to Chapter 1: An (Accepting) Audience of One.

Some authors write prose that is truly remarkable to read. It's beautiful. People *do* come to those authors' books to revel in the prose. But many of us would do better to let the story and characters, not stellar sentences, be in the spotlight.

How do you step into the background and let your story take center stage? I've got some suggestions and preferences here, but they're not "laws." Use them if you agree, and don't worry if you don't.

First, keep your vocabulary "normal." You don't want to dumb down your writing, nor should you attempt to raise it artificially. Try to keep it within the bounds of what a typical member of your target audience would understand.

Second, avoid the bizarre turn of phrase. You want to avoid cliché and pursue originality but not to the extent that it draws attention to itself. Any time you make the reader focus on the words you're using, as opposed to the story you're telling, you snap her out of the illusion that she's *in* the story.

Third, stick to *said*. Don't say, "'That's fine,' she breathed." Or, "'That stinks,' she pondered." Or, "'Okay by me,' she laughed." Don't let characters sigh, chortle, postulate, surmise, heave, opine, verbalize, snipe, deride, or question words out. All that does is draw attention to your interjections, in my opinion.

Said is invisible. Invisible is good—it's what you're striving for. *Asked* is okay, too (as in "'Is that yours?' she asked"), but almost everything else is blatantly visible and can knock the reader out of your story.

What you want is a reader who is enthralled by your story so that she forgets she's reading words and turning pages. You want her breathlessly moving beyond the sentences and directly into the front row of the story. Your words cease to be ends in and of themselves, instead becoming the vehicle that conveys her into the reality you've created.

When that happens, she'll get to the end of your book and look at the clock, only to realize with surprise that it's three in the morning.

chapter 4
UNDERSTAND YOUR CALLING AS A NOVELIST

As a Christian you are called to minister to two main groups of people: those inside the Church and those outside it. You have responsibilities toward both groups.

However, I believe each Christian may be *primarily* called to one group or the other. For instance, those Christians with the spiritual gift of evangelism are going to be spending most of their time focused on people outside the Church. Those Christians with the gift of pastoring will be more focused on people inside the Church.

No matter your gift or calling, you cannot neglect either group. Just because you feel called to the Church doesn't mean you can neglect missionary work, for instance, or vice versa.

When it comes to Christian writers—and Christian novelists, in particular—I believe a similar distinction applies. Christian novelists have a responsibility toward those people inside the Church and those outside it but *are primarily called to one or the other.*

You probably know which calling God has placed on your life. If your heart beats to reach non-Christians through your fiction, then that's a clear indicator you're called to write your fiction primarily for that group. When I began writing, my father was not a Christian, so I wrote my first trilogy as a form of apologetics. If, on the other hand, you find your groove when challenging and entertaining fellow Christians, you're probably called to write primarily for those inside the Church.

I don't understand why Christian novelists get into arguments about this, but I see such exchanges regularly. One person feels called to Group A and insists that everyone ought to be called to Group A. But another person feels just as strongly that Group B is where everyone should be devoting their energies.

This is similar to the early church getting mad at Paul for taking the gospel to the Gentiles when the apostles all thought the good news was primarily for the Jews. They finally decided to stop fighting God and let each party take the gospel to the group each one had been called to.

So it should be with Christian novelists. So it should be with you.

It's okay if everyone doesn't feel called to the same group you feel called to. I know it's a big job reaching the lost or edifying the Church, but it really is all right if some of the effort goes to the other group. Particularly if your best efforts seem to be directed in that particular area.

So do you have a feel for which group you're called to? Do you write for the lost or the Church? Or is there a third group you feel led to reach? Or maybe you feel called to one group now, but in years past you felt called to the other. That's fine.

For example, Marcher Lord Press is dedicated to reaching a subset of the Church: those Christians who love speculative fiction but are not currently being served by the CBA publishing industry. (*CBA* stands for Christian Booksellers Association and is a shorthand way of referring to the Christian publishing industry in North America.) I'll also be pleased if non-Christians discover Marcher Lord Press and find their way to salvation through it, but that's not my primary focus.

For whom do you write? Your lost relative and those like her? Your prodigal son and those like him? A particular group or subculture? Praise God for your calling, whatever it is!

If you don't know your calling as a novelist, ask God. You'll probably realize that you've known all along. Or you may discover that your calling changes over time. Either way, He'll guide you.

WRITING AND PUBLISHING FOR THE CHURCH

Once you know for whom you're writing, you'll have a good idea about what to put in your fiction and where to look when it's time to seek publication. When you know your target audience, you know how to write. You know what kind of stories will appeal to that group and what their issues are. An author trying to write for all groups simultaneously usually ends up unhappy (and unpublished).

I recommend getting a photo of your ideal reader and pasting that photo up on your computer monitor. As you're writing, keep glancing at that person's face; imagine that you're crafting this story specifically for him or her. If you do, your story will be well suited to both your target reader and all the people *like* that reader.

When it comes time to think about publication for your novel, your calling comes into play, too.

If you're writing to the Church, then your publishing choices are clear: The CBA publishing industry is where you'll go. There are hundreds of Christian publishing companies that do a very good job of reaching the Church. Most of the Church, that is.

If you're called to write to a part of the Church that the CBA doesn't serve, your choices are more limited. If you want your fiction to reach Christian men, for instance, you're basically out of luck. If you want your fiction to reach Christians who love Tom Clancy, David Eddings, or Ian Fleming, you're in trouble.

As I explain later in this book, we're living in the midst of a publishing revolution in which virtually every kind of Christian fiction is finding its audience. But aside from Marcher Lord Press and a handful of others, the revolution hasn't spread far yet. You may have to wait for the market to catch up to you.

In the meantime, keep writing! When the right publishing avenue presents itself, it will be great for you to have several completed novels ready to go.

WRITING AND PUBLISHING FOR NON-CHRISTIANS

If you feel called to write to a non-Christian readership, I have some bad news for you: The Christian publishing industry doesn't reach non-Christians. It just doesn't.

Yes, I know CBA publishers are getting Christian books into Sam's, Walmart, and Barnes & Noble. But, in my experience, non-Christians are not buying these books. Christians are purchasing them because they are looking for the reduced prices they can find at these stores.

It's undoubtedly true that some non-Christians picked up Christian fiction in these venues and that God has done amazing things with them. The Left Behind phenomenon certainly brought in a lot of curious people from outside the Church. But, by and large, Christian publishers sell to Christians.

Where are Christian novels shelved in Barnes & Noble? In the general-fiction shelves? In romance, science fiction, historical? Not so much. Most are put in the religious-fiction area. I like to call this Death Row because who even goes to those shelves? Non-Christians? Not likely.

If God has called you to write to non-Christians, you may be looking at non-Christian publishers for your fiction.

This is a sticky wicket. Most of the Christian novelists I know who feel called to write to non-Christians have not fully figured it out. How do you get Christian stories into the hands of non-Christians?

If you go through an American Book Association (ABA) publisher ("ABA" is a way to refer to secular publishers, just as "CBA" is shorthand to refer to Christian publishers), won't you be forced to remove specifically Christian content? Worse, won't you be forced to include content that would be offensive to Christians?

There's no single answer to this. Some ABA publishers are exactly like this. Some are not. Some are so enamored with the idea of spirituality in fiction that they'll ask you to include more explicitly Christian content.

Or perhaps you should go a more covert route: Make Christianity an underlying theme, or write an allegory. Many people allege the screenplay for *E.T.* was a veiled depiction of the life, death, and resurrection of Jesus Christ. Maybe that's the way you should go.

Perhaps the same advice mentioned above applies to you: The publishing revolution we're in allows you to bypass all these artificial categories and simply distribute your books to anyone who will like them, Christian or not. When you no longer have to identify your faith by walking into a particular bookstore or a section of a bookstore, you can buy whatever kind of book you please. That will be a good day for Christian novelists who are called to write to non-Christians, though challenges still remain in grabbing readers' attention.

THE BETTER QUESTION

Was Jesus called to those inside the family of faith or those outside? I think we'd have to say both. He was called to Israel, but He spent most of His time with those who had been spurned by "good Jews." He came to the Jews, but His ministry clearly extended to those from other flocks.

When Jesus spoke to His disciples, He taught with parables (fiction) and straightforward teaching. When He stood in the marketplace, he taught in parables (fiction) to fish for men and reel them in to hear straight teaching.

No matter your calling as a novelist, and no matter the path God uses to get your writing to His intended audience, you have to do just one thing: Keep writing. Keep telling these stories as if they're reaching your ideal reader and all those like her. Be wise. Think about strategies and avenues to get your stuff out there. Write well and with precision to your calling.

But in the end you must let God be in charge of taking your fish and loaves and multiplying them out to the people He knows need them.

chapter 5
BE TEACHABLE

In publishing, as in all corners of life, God opposes the proud and gives grace to the humble. An attitude of humility before God and others will serve you well as you pursue a career in Christian fiction publishing.

Most of the aspiring Christian novelists I know are wonderful, humble people. They are eager to learn and dogged in their commitment to apply what they learn. It is their goal to raise their craftsmanship to the point where their fiction will be considered publishable.

Such people are a joy to work with.

Writers' conferences are full of these kinds of folk. They're serious about wanting to improve and are willing to invest in their own education and improvement. This is one of the reasons I work so hard at writers' conferences, helping and advising where I can, even as I feel overwhelmed and sometimes bled dry. What teacher wouldn't knock himself out to help eager learners?

But occasionally I run into an aspiring novelist who doesn't want to learn anything more.

Such folks usually indicate that they think their prose is golden as it is. They feel they've already read everything they need to read and learned every technique worth learning. And they believe their story is from God Himself. Every word. Does God need an editor? Does God need instruction?

This kind of attitude is less pleasurable to encounter.

Chances are, you're going to have to make a lot of changes to get your novel published. It may have "just come to you," but that doesn't mean it's well written. You may have written it in an altered state of consciousness, as if God were downloading it directly to your brain, but that doesn't mean it's ready to be published. Or even that it *was* from God and not the result of the mysterious psychological machinations in your own mind.

No one can deny that Saul, later the Apostle Paul, had a direct experience with God. And yet he took off into the desert for years to figure out Christianity before he was ready. He realized that an encounter with God did not mean he shouldn't also seek preparation.

Maewyn Succat, better known as Saint Patrick, received a bonafide vision from God to return to Ireland to bring the Gospel to his former captors. But he took several years in ecclesiastical training before he set out.

A calling is essential, but it's not the only thing. Training is also needed. And you can't be trained if you're not teachable.

I also encounter this attitude from a different group of would-be Christian novelists: "Craft? Who needs to learn craft?" These are the folks who have sugarcoated a sermon, designed to knock readers upside the head, into fiction. Agenda-driven novelists don't often want to bother learning the craft of fiction. They're just dipping into fiction long enough to disguise their +2 mace of bludgeoning.

Don't be like this. No one wants to invalidate the authenticity of your vision, and I acknowledge that your book could really be directly from God. But do you want to get it published or not?

WEIGHING THE OPTIONS

Long before I actually got published with Multnomah, I *almost* got published with Zondervan. I had this series of fantasy novels I wanted to write, and the fiction editor there at the time (the blessed St. Dave Lambert) was interested in the series.

But he thought it would work better as a Young Adult series (for fourteen- to eighteen-year-olds).

How interested was I in getting published? In my mind, this was a serious series for adults. Would I be willing to bend my original idea in order to get published? Or was I going to hold on to my vision and later console myself with the satisfaction that I had at least stuck to my guns?

I told him a YA series would be boffo. Sweet. Let's do it.

I was willing to make that compromise, to be teachable. As it turned out, Zondervan eventually decided they didn't even want it as a YA series, but the point remains.

Years later, after my first trilogy had been published by Multnomah, I sent out a proposal for another novel. This one was for a book I called *Grasping at Angels.* (You can still read the opening chapters at my website: www.JeffersonScott.com.)

It was a hard sell in many ways. In fact, it was probably the best thing you could put together if you wanted to *not* get published in CBA. It was a tragic, male-oriented story about a poor serf in an unpopular era of history, and it didn't even have any romance in it. And I wrote it in present tense.

I sent that proposal out far and wide. Acquisitions editors around the industry said they liked the writing but there was basically no way they could get the thing published.

Again, along came the aforementioned St. Lambert. Dave looked at the proposal and said it might have a better chance if it were in past tense.

How interested was I in getting this thing published? I had my reasons for using present tense, but I knew it was unconventional, especially way back in the late '90s. And here I had industry pros telling me it was one of the obstacles to getting the book published. Would I stick to my original vision or be teachable and bow to the wisdom of these people?

I rewrote it in past tense.

Even so, all those publishers eventually decided not to publish it. Ow. But it was another opportunity for me to show whether or not I would harden my neck against reproof.

How about you? You probably feel you're as humble as a kitten, but what have your actions shown? Has an industry veteran recommended a change to your book, and yet you've felt your neck tighten against even considering one more change?

When you decide you don't want to make the change an industry insider recommends (whether you think the person is right or not, and whatever your reasons for doing so), what you're usually saying is that you'd rather not be published at the moment.

When you decide to stick to your artistic vision, that's a legitimate choice. Just don't complain that the book continues to be rejected. Yes, maybe it is because the entire industry is broken and every editor is shortsighted. But it might also be because you don't yet know enough about the industry or your craft. It might serve you better to remain teachable.

BILL AND TED STRIKE AGAIN

My beloved Bill S. Preston, Esquire, once encountered an idea from Socratic philosophy: "The only true wisdom consists in knowing that you know nothing." To which the venerable Ted "Theodore" Logan responded, "That's us, dude!"

Amen, brethren.

I hope you never reach the point where you decide you've learned enough and don't need to learn anything else.

Certain novelists get so famous that they are allowed to reject their editors' every suggestion. Some don't even use editors. And some publishers let them get away with it because they know the book is going to sell whether it's been edited or not.

I hope you never get there, even if you become a best-selling author ten times over.

You will always lose objectivity about your own writing. You will always have something you can improve in your craft. And you will always need humility in this and every aspect of your life.

Stay teachable, my friend. (And party on, dude!)

chapter 6
STOP BEING TEACHABLE

This topic serves as a nice transition from the spiritual aspects of writing to the practical. At some point, you do have to move out of intake mode and into output mode.

Let me be sure I'm very clear in what I mean here. You should never stop being teachable. Ever. It's an attitude of humility that must characterize every portion of your life, especially your writing.

But in the craft of fiction writing there are times when you must decide it's time to stop taking instruction and start writing. It doesn't mean you've stopped being humble before God and men. It just means it's time to apply what you've learned so far.

BUILDING YOUR OWN LIGHTSABER

I see this at writers' conferences. Attendees from one of my classes come up and tell me, "You say we should avoid backstory in our fiction, but in the seminar next door they're saying we should include it. What gives?" Or, "You say stick to *said*, but the teacher last year said *said* is boring. What should I do?"

Sometimes these poor people can get so wound up in trying to do what every writing teacher says that they can't move. Because not every person who teaches fiction writing agrees with everyone else who teaches fiction writing. Yet the aspiring writer doesn't want to violate any rule of fiction.

These folks can find themselves in the unenviable position of trying to simultaneously adhere to opposing teachings. Psychologists call that *cognitive dissonance,* and it's a good way to drive yourself crazy.

Here's a helpful piece of advice for you, inspired by our sixteenth president: You can't please all the fiction-writing teachers all the time.

These jokers (myself included) all have their own sets of rules, likes, dislikes, and pet peeves. They each have their own schools of thought about what makes good fiction. You can't possibly adhere to them all, because they don't agree with each other.

So what do you do?

You sift through all the "truths" about fiction writing you hear, and you hang on to the ones that make sense to you.

If one person says no jumping to a second story line within the first forty pages (that's me!), and another person says you should have at least three story lines going by page 40, you've got to put your brain into gear and figure out which one seems right to you.

Investigate. Try both ways. Look for examples of both. Look at the reasoning behind both teachings. Look at the fiction produced by both teachers. Decide which one to go with.

When you do this, you are, in a sense, ceasing to be teachable. You're saying, "Wait a minute, I can't do both of these. Which one am I going to go with?" You're ceasing to be the yes-sir/yes-ma'am writing pupil and are beginning to, if you'll allow the *Star Wars* reference, build your own lightsaber.

That's what we're talking about here. We're talking about you figuring out what kind of writer you want to be. You're deciding which option you prefer in dozens of stylistic choices.

Maybe you don't like *said*, but you do like cutting out backstory. That's okay. Go for it. Maybe you decide that only first person and present tense will ever work for you, no matter what anyone says. Awesome. Take your shot and carve out your niche. Decide who you want to be. Not in the defiant in-your-face sense but in the sense of a teenager figuring out what kind of adult she wants to be.

You will come to the time when the childhood days of instruction are finished and the adult days of productivity are upon you.

You're able to craft what kind of novelist you want to be. What will that look like for you?

COUNT THE COST

One word of warning: As soon as you stop agreeing with every teacher or book on writing, you're going to start being in disagreement with many of them.

That's part of maturation, too. You can't please everyone and be a good writer.

If you want to keep pleasing everyone, stick with the yes-ma'am stuff and continue revising (or reversing) your writing style with every new writing teacher you study under. That's a legitimate part of the learning process.

But when you're ready to plant your stake and say, "No, *this* is the kind of writer I want to be," brace yourself for opposition.

What if you love backstory and have decided that the first twenty pages of every book you write will be nothing but the life stories of your main characters? Well, if that's what you want to do, go for it. But if you're asking an agent to represent you or an editor to publish you, you'd better hope that person loves frontl-oaded novels, too, or you're going to get rejected.

It goes back to my question: How badly do you want to be published? Are you willing to compromise some of your line-in-the-sand stylistic preferences to get published at a house that doesn't like what you've decided to do in your fiction? Or would you rather keep looking and possibly not get published with this project?

Some other writer who is happy to revise her book according to the preferences of the agent or editor may find herself published long before you are. That's the risk you take when you decide your way is the only way you can write.

The phases are like this: When you start out writing fiction, you're basically a child. Hopefully you're extremely teachable in this phase. You have to realize you know nothing about writing and must be willing to learn from those who do. Your writing will forever be infantile if you don't.

Then you enter the teenage phase of a writer's development. Here you're starting to realize that not every expert is infallible and agrees with every other expert. You're beginning to disagree with some experts and to develop a whole toolbox full of techniques and styles you prefer. There's a sense of mild rebellion here as you begin to feel more certain of what you like and who you want to be as a writer. That's good and normal.

The final phase of a writer's development (if there is such a thing) is the equivalent of adulthood. You've achieved some measure of success. You've found a whole bunch of things that seem to work for you.

You're still learning, you're still experimenting, you're still challenging yourself, but most of the growth and development is behind you. You know who you are as a writer, and you're confident in that. You may even be in a position to teach others.

But even in this last phase you must remain teachable. Nobody likes a know-it-all, even if she's a successful novelist. Everybody must keep growing, and an attitude of humility is essential in the Christian life.

BUT YOU ARE NOT A JEDI YET

Is my own writing perfect? Hardly. Is it a reflection of what I'm attempting? Yes. Am I pleased with my style? Have I found my voice? Yes and yes. Can I learn new things and improve areas of my craftsmanship? Absolutely.

At this point in my writing life, I look to peers and to other novelists I admire, including some secular authors and some authors of the classics. I examine their styles or teachings to see if there are aspects of them that could improve my own fiction. But those things must fit into my overall sense of who I am as a novelist.

And honestly, I'm not looking too hard. I'm pleased with what I'm doing, and I feel I'm more or less done with the major writing lessons in my life. Hopefully I have remained humble and teachable as a person and as a writer. But I'm also confident enough in what I'm capable of that I've stopped reading books on how to get better as a writer.

What you're looking for in *your* development is the same thing. You need to go through all the phases, and you need to remain teachable. But you're heading to the place where you know what to do and how to do it, and you're happy with how it comes out on the page. You realize you may need to change this or that to meet the approval of an agent or editor, but you're not going to automatically make that change just because. You may decide to pass.

You're headed to a place of satisfied confidence in your writing. In one facet of craft after another you'll realize you've reached a place of sufficient skill and don't need to hear any new opinions about it, at least for now. Maybe later you'll change your mind. You can always remain humble while at the same time ending the phase of basic learning.

Be teachable, except when you stop. And even when you stop being teachable, stay teachable.

CONCLUDING PART I

Anybody can sit down and try to write a novel. Many people can actually accomplish it. But only the Christian novelist comes at fiction with the mind of Christ.

It's important to get the first things first. Your heart must be right before God as you approach anything you do, including writing fiction, if you are to be a conduit for His power.

I pray that you and I will both get out of the way and let God's words shine through as we write. And I pray that we will become better craftspeople, always humble, able to bring God an offering worthy of His name.

PART II

STRATEGIZING YOURSELF, STRATEGIZING YOUR NOVEL

chapter 7

CHANGE THE METAPHOR YOU USE FOR YOURSELF AS A NOVELIST

In Part II we will look at overarching things pertaining to your book: three-act structure, character creation, and other story-related topics that you need to figure out before you even start. Strategic-level matters.

We will also cover two strategic things about you as a novelist. In the next chapter, we'll talk about whether you should write what you want or what the market wants. In this one we'll talk about how to think of yourself as a writer.

PASS THE S'MORES

You're not a storyteller spinning yarns beside a campfire.

You're not. You can't think of yourself that way. Many novelists do think of themselves in that way, but I'm here to tell you that such a metaphor will give rise to a number of errors in your fiction.

At least, those would be errors in the sort of fiction I personally prefer. I'm no longer willing to say that something in fiction is an error so long as it doesn't make the reader stop reading. Keep that in mind as you read.

In a real sense, you certainly are a storyteller. What is a novelist if not a storyteller? But you are not the guy sitting on a log captivating your audience of marshmallow-roasting listeners with your tale of romance or adventure.

Because when you think of yourself like this, you are going to do things in your writing that you shouldn't do. You're going to explain everything, for starters. You're going to give backstory and shortcuts that help your listener but don't help a reader.

> Now, Jake was a vile man. He'd killed three men with his bare hands in a barroom brawl, and he liked to beat up old ladies because they usually had a bit of jewelry he could steal.

Something like that would work around a campfire. But in fiction, it's called *telling*. You want to focus on *showing*. We'll talk about showing versus telling in more detail in Part III.

If you think of yourself as a storyteller around a campfire, you're also going to summarize everything.

> Jake moved through the wagon train, beating up old ladies, until he'd stolen every last piece of jewelry in the group. After that, he cooked the ox and had himself a fine steak dinner.

With a few lines of text I've relayed something that should've been detailed in a full scene or even multiple scenes. The storyteller metaphor encourages this kind of summary while simultaneously discouraging good fiction technique.

Here's another reason to change your metaphor: If you think of yourself as a storyteller around the campfire, you're likely to violate point-of-view rules.

> Jake slept off his ox-steak dinner. Then, unbeknownst to him, but knownst to us, Mary Ellen and Becky Sue got the womenfolk together to come up with a plan. Mary Ellen was in favor of shooting the snake because she'd had a no-good husband like Jake once't before. Becky Sue was more of a mind to tie him up to a cactus, being of a more kindly nature and wishing to extend the love of Jesus to him, though she knew he truly was a snake.

You can't go hopping into everyone's head. It works at the Kampgrounds of America (K.O.A.) or summer camp. Not so much in a novel.

If you think of yourself as a storyteller around a campfire, you also won't give proper descriptions of places, people, or events. You might mention "the barn," but you probably won't describe it as you should. Readers need sensory information, establishing shots, comparisons, and the rest. You probably won't share the crucial details that sell it to the reader.

In short, without making adjustments, even the best campfire storytellers make lousy novelists.

WHAT, THEN?

If you're not a fireside storyteller, what are you? What should your metaphor be for yourself as a novelist?

You must cease thinking of yourself as a fireside tale-teller and begin thinking of yourself as a *filmmaker.*

Now the scenario has changed. You're limited to camera and microphone to convey your story. You have to dress your characters and light your scene and compose your shots. You are forced to *show* the story through action, scene, and dialogue.

A filmmaker can't just summarize a scene—she has to play it out blow by blow and shot by shot. A filmmaker can't just suggest a setting—she has to build it. She can't just assume the audience is going to imagine things happening in the background—she's got to put them there.

When you're a filmmaker you can't *tell* anymore, as you can by the campfire. Now you're forced to use good fiction techniques. You have to pick whose story this is, so you can't go head-hopping. Your characters can't be random blobs, as they could be in a storyteller's tale; they have to be precisely selected actors.

If you begin thinking of yourself as a filmmaker, someone whose story can be told *only* through the filmmaker's tools, your fiction will instantly improve. You'll be less inclined to fall into bad habits, and your stories will take on a new visual quality they hadn't had before.

It might help you to read a book on basic filmmaking. Better yet, break out the video camera and make a simple movie. You'll discover that you need to be close in for some things and far away for others. You'll understand the need for an establishing shot. And you'll see why you have to establish who is in a scene if you want to use them later, or else they'll appear to materialize from nowhere.

And if you're really paying attention, you'll begin to see what telling is like. In a movie, telling would be like making the screen go black for twenty minutes while some boring narrator fills the viewer in about backstory.

You would never make a movie like that. And yet beginning novelists do it all the time. They stop their story, making the reader stare at a blank screen, while they explain the universe, the history between characters, and everything else. This doesn't work in a movie, and it doesn't work in fiction.

The filmmaker metaphor will help you on so many levels. It's almost like the ultimate fiction secret.

So toss aside your s'mores and put on your director's chapeau. It's time to stop telling stories and start making movies—on paper.

chapter 8

SHOULD YOU WRITE WHAT YOU WANT OR WHAT THE MARKET WANTS?

The first strategic question about your book is what metaphor you should use about yourself as the author. The second strategic question is whether you should write to the market or stick to the crazy ideas bouncing around in your head.

I get this question a lot. Aspiring authors hear through the grapevine that Christian fiction publishers are sick of a certain genre, which usually happens to be the genre they're writing. Or publishers are eager to buy manuscripts in some other genre, which the author had never considered writing. The angst begins.

Should I ditch what I'm doing and write to what publishers want right now? Or should I keep writing this novel, even though it goes against the grain? What if I start writing in this new genre, and by the time I get a novel finished, they've changed what they want again?

My counsel is this: Write what you want. Write what you have a passion to write because it's passion, not market savvy or the thought of hitting an acquirer at the right time. This will propel you through the lonely marathon that is writing a novel. What should you write? You should write the story that *must* come out of you because it's burning a hole in your heart.

Now, lest I sound like a Pollyanna, let me say if you do soldier on and write the novel of your heart, it doesn't mean you'll be able to sell it to a publisher. You may find yourself content but unpublished (which, as it turns out, is not that bad a thing).

There are market realities, you see. Writing something that is contrary to these realities is a good way to remain unpublished. But at least you'll have finished the book of your heart.

It is true that the market changes. But it drives me crazy when I hear that the editors at a publishing company are looking only for novels in genre X and aspiring authors go nuts trying to jump through that hoop.

If you're thinking like this, I urge you to consider that this desperation may not be of God. To me, changing yourself to try to fit the shifting demands of a fickle marketplace isn't right. Better to find out how God wants you to be and let the vagaries of "demand" cascade around you like the proverbial chips falling where they may.

Now, if you happen to have a completed manuscript in the genre that's supposedly hot, you're golden. Just have your agent send it to the acquisitions editor in question. (More about agents and completed manuscripts in Chapter 53.) Striking while the iron is hot doesn't guarantee you'll be published, but you may find your proposal arrives at the right place at the right time. Then you will be glad you went ahead and persevered in writing that novel, even though no one was buying fiction in that genre at the time.

But if you don't have a novel in the allegedly hot genre, don't drop what you're doing and start trying to write one. When I was writing the first version of this book (early 2009), Amish fiction was all the rage in Christian publishing. How many novelists decided to try their hand at bonnet-and-buggy fiction to catch the wave? Crazy.

(The Amish fiction fad ended up lasting several years, to my chagrin. But I showed them: I published *Amish Vampires in Space* in 2013.)

Unless we're talking about one of the genres that the core CBA readership will always love, you may find the landscape has changed by the time you arrive with a finished manuscript. Then you'll be more disheartened than ever.

Write the story of your heart. Write what you love, what you have a passion for. If your story is in some genre that is way off the edge of the map, you may find it more difficult to get a publisher interested. But that passion will come through on the page, which is worth any amount of fad chasing. And it's just possible that the market will eventually come around to you—at which time you'll have a manuscript all ready to go.

It's also feasible that new publishing venues will open up that will be interested in your novel, such as what happened to authors of Christian speculative fiction when I launched Marcher Lord Press.

Trust that the story that has captured you is a story God would love to have you write. Then you'll be back to the very first tip of all: writing for an accepting audience of One.

chapter 9

HOW TO FIND YOUR STORY

We turn now from strategizing yourself as a novelist to strategizing your book. Here we talk about plot, character, and other aspects of your book that need to be figured out before you type your first word on the screen. We'll also come to the first of five "Focus on the Craft" sections in *The Art & Craft of Writing Christian Fiction.*

Before you write your book, it's good if you know more or less what it's going to be, wouldn't you agree? You don't need to preplan everything. But you should know what genre you're going to write in, who your main character is, and some broad brushstrokes of the story you're about to write.

How do you find your story?

Does that strike you as an odd question? You've got things happening, people doing things, lots of scenes, dialogue, description, and stuff. How can you not have your story?

I'm here to tell you that, as a book doctor, I am often dealing with manuscripts in which the author has not found his story. The manuscript may be 250,000 words long, but the story is not there. (Indeed, the authors of most 250,000-word manuscripts have *not* found their stories.)

The story meanders and never finds its way. The ending has nothing to do with the beginning or even with the main character. The protagonist has no quest or arc. There are no stakes, or the stakes don't show up until the last 20 percent of the manuscript.

If that weren't enough, these manuscripts are often plagued with gobs of writing problems, such as telling, interchangeable characters, poor dialogue, a lack of description, an almost complete lack of structure, and pretty much everything else this book sets out to rectify. (Lots more on fixing these writing problems in Part III.)

How do you know if you haven't found your story? Well, a bloated, overly long manuscript is one indicator. Having agents or editors reject your manuscript may be another. Hearing from readers that they got bored is a clue. Feeling in your own heart that something may be wrong, even though you can't put your finger on it, might be a sign.

Whether you feel like you've captured your story or not, it will help you to go through these steps.

IT ALL STARTS WITH CHARACTER

That might surprise you to read, coming from a plot-first novelist like me. But in my experience I have come to realize that character really is the starting point.

You've got a setting, a premise, and probably some pretty strong plot ideas. That's normal and good. But in terms of figuring out how to tell that story in the best way, it all starts with character.

Who is your main character? Do you know? Who do you *want* it to be?

Ask yourself what this character is like. Have you done your homework to figure out who this person is, what she wants, and where she is going in this story? Until you know these things, you are doomed to wander around in a storyless, unpublished wilderness.

But when you *do* figure this out, you're at least 75 percent of the way to finding your story. Truly, your main character's inner journey is the largest component of your story.

Or, rather, it should be.

Then when you figure out the inner journeys of your antagonist and two to four other major characters in your book, you'll be about 80 percent of the way to knowing your story.

There. Wasn't that easy? Figure out your characters, and you'll be most of the way to figuring out your story.

DETERMINE THE STAKES

After determining your main character's inner journey, only a few things are lacking—at least percentage-wise.

The first of these is the "or else" component of your book. What are the stakes? What will happen if the antagonist gets his way, and the protagonist is unsuccessful in stopping it? This is what I call the ticking time bomb (more on this in Chapter 18).

The ticking time bomb is something the reader knows about very early in the story, even if the protagonist doesn't find out about it until later. Every page the reader turns brings her that much closer to doom.

The first season of the TV show *Heroes* has a great example of a ticking time bomb. The characters are in October, but they discover that on November 8 a nuclear bomb will destroy New York City. Viewers (and soon, the characters) learn about this early on, and every episode takes them closer to that detonation—unless our "heroes" can save the day.

Figure out what this ticking time bomb will be in your tale, and then establish it early. Once you do, you'll have about 90 percent of the story.

FIND YOUR THREE-ACT STRUCTURE

When you know your characters' journeys and the "or else" eventuality they're working to prevent, you're almost home. The last big chunk of it is to determine what your book's structure will be.

You don't have to feel like you're mapping your book out in too much detail or that you'll be bound to this structure once you start writing. But having an idea of the major chunks of your story will help you as you write—especially if you're a character-first novelist.

As we've seen, the filmmaking metaphor is useful when talking about fiction. Most screenwriters speak in terms of Act 1, Act 2, and Act 3. Screenwriting books use this convention. It's helpful for novelists, too.

- Act 1—introductions and setup: everything up to the point where the hero decides to commit to the problem
- Act 2—the heart of the story: everything from there to the point when the thing happens that initiates the story's climactic series of events
- Act 3—rising action, the climax, and the dénouement: everything from there to the end

The thing to remember is that you're looking for a single watershed event that marks the end of one act and the beginning of the next. The transition from Act 1 to Act 2 in almost all stories is the moment when all the lead-up and setup is complete, and the hero makes the decision to engage the issue. It's the "enough is enough" moment.

Let's use the movie *Alien* for discussion. In my opinion, Act 1 would end when the alien bursts out of Cain's chest, hisses, and slithers away. Now the main story really begins: the struggle of the alien against the crew. The crew begins taking action to hunt the alien down and kill it. This is the heart of the story and the content of Act 2. Whatever moment that transition happened—from wondering what's going on to trying to kill the alien and surviving—is the transition from Act 1 to Act 2.

The transition from Act 2 to Act 3 is usually clearer. Act 2 is well underway, with everything moving toward the climactic showdown. There comes a moment in Act 2 when all the pieces are in place for the final confrontation. When that moment comes, you've transitioned from Act 2 to Act 3.

In *Alien,* Act 3 begins when the alien has killed all the crew except Ripley. It's down to the two of them. The moment of truth is at hand. Ripley is our viewpoint character, our surrogate, so it's really down to that thing and *us.* The moment the last crewmember dies is the moment when everything is set up for a final confrontation. That's the transition from Act 2 to Act 3.

To recap: Act 1 is prologue to "the main story." The transition between Act 1 and Act 2 is when the hero engages this main issue—or it engages him. Act 1 may take up a lot of time in the story, or it may not. In my novels, Act 1 typically takes up the first half of the book.

Act 2 is the main story: the juicy parts, the reason you wanted to write this book in the first place. It is everything up until the moment when the final confrontation is set up and ready to play out.

That confrontation and the rest of the story is Act 3.

In a sense, Act 1 is setup for Act 2, the main story, and Act 2 is setup for Act 3, the huge confrontation. The events of the story have been rushing toward this confrontation from the first page.

In my novel *Operation: Firebrand—Crusade*, the Firebrand team has been sent to Sudan to rescue some villagers who have been abducted and sold into slavery. Act 1 covers everything from the beginning up to the moment when the team realizes the situation is much worse than they'd thought. They have a conscience check when they ask themselves if they really can just leave the rest of these people to their abductors. They decide to stay and really hurt these slavers. That decision marks the transition from Act 1 to Act 2.

Act 2 is the "crusade" of the title. It's why I wrote the book. Everything before was just the setup for this crusade. It's the heart of the story.

We're in Act 2 right up until the moment when the Firebrand team is betrayed and used as bait for the enemy force. This last battle (a fight for survival) is the final confrontation of the story; it is the climax. That segment of the story, plus the resolution and dénouement, is Act 3.

What is your story's three-act structure? When you know your characters' inner journeys and you know what the ticking time bomb is, you're ready to determine how to fit these into three acts.

When you do that, you'll have found 95 percent of your story.

AND THE REST

The last 5 percent consists of genre, setting, era, backdrop, your theme or message (if any), and sundry subplots.

So if you believe your story is foundering, or if you've been told you haven't found your story (or if you just want to be sure you have the story you think you have), be sure you have these things in place.

Who is your protagonist, and what is his inner journey? What does your protagonist want—and what is the ticking time bomb he is trying to prevent? What is a good three-act structure in which to convey those things?

Determine these items, and you will have found your story.

Focus on the Craft: CHARACTER

When it comes to writing Christian fiction there are a few topics that require special attention. In my "Fiction Writing Tip of the Week" column, these were the topics I came back to again and again, wrote series of tips about, or both. The topics were so important and had so many facets that they merited this kind of prolonged discussion.

For *The Art & Craft of Writing Christian Fiction*, I have grouped these thoughts into sections that focus on the craft of writing.

The first group we'll talk about concerns character creation. If, as Chapter 12 will suggest, your main character and her inner journey constitute 75 percent of your story, it makes sense to look at character right away.

chapter 10

CREATE INTERESTING CHARACTERS (WHO DON'T ALL SOUND LIKE YOU)

When you think of your favorite novels, what do you think of? Is it a climactic moment, a thrill of action, or an amazing and strange world? Possibly. But I'll bet that right at the top of the list is a favorite character.

What is *Star Wars* without Han Solo? What is *Lord of the Rings* without Gollum? What is *Minority Report* without Agatha? What is *The Once and Future King* without Merlin? What is *Lord of the Flies* without Piggy and Jack and Simon and Samneric? What is *O Brother, Where Art Thou* without … well, without any of those guys?

Think of the incredible characters in TV shows like *Battlestar Galactica, Lost, Grey's Anatomy, Friends*, and *Monk*. If you're like me, it's not long before you're coming back to the show not for the story, the humor, or anything else, but to find out what happens next with your favorite characters. You just want to hang with them. You miss them.

Long after we forget the good feelings a work of fiction produces in us, after we forget the great special effects or the magnificent cinematography or the stirring soundtrack, we are left with the resonance of great characters.

Strong, believable, fully realized characters make your fiction memorable. Even if you have the most brilliant premise, the best craftsmanship, and the most wonderful cover design in the world, characters will separate your fiction from the pack.

The converse is also true. Without characters of that caliber, a great premise, high craftsmanship, and a terrific cover will not save your book from the fate of being only "pretty good."

There are some novels that have been huge hits, though they have very shallow characters. This would seem to invalidate what I'm saying here, but it doesn't. Those books are a flash in the pan. They will not remain perennial favorites among readers. They tend to get hot because of some scandal, fad, or timeliness. But it will not last.

The only thing that will make your fiction endure will be excellent characters.

ME NOT DO CHARACTERS GOOD

Before you read any of this you were probably already convinced that you needed great characters for your fiction.

But here's where you may be stymied. You know you need to create these immortals to strut about your stage, but maybe you don't know how. You realize that you can come up with story ideas or cool plot elements all day long, but you couldn't write a decent character to save your life.

I see this all the time in the unpublished fiction manuscripts I work with. I often see manuscripts in which the author thinks his characters are believable so long as they have different moods or agendas. No matter that they all seem and sound the same (just like the author) in every substantive way.

Jenny might be a widow, Frida a gold digger, and Laura a haggard soccer mom, but they all still sound too much like the author. Then you've got mean Jimmy, rich Harry, and nice Larry. Those are not memorable characters. And yet most novels I see are populated with such nonentities. It's as if cardboard cutouts have come to life and are floating around the stage spouting one-liners.

This kind of half-baked character creation is the result of either laziness or ignorance. Either the author doesn't realize that his characters all sound the same, except for attitude or role, or he doesn't want to do the hard work of making the characters different and realistic.

Such characters are probably the work of plot-first novelists. These writers, the fellowship of which I am a card-carrying member, tend to create awful characters. Other writers, character-first novelists, come up with great characters but usually don't know what to have them do.

In a plot-first novelist's book, the characters almost always sound the same, act the same, and *seem* the same. They have different attitudes or goals, but it's more like the same person just being mad, jealous, conniving, or whatever. They're like clone troopers with different-colored helmets. And not only do they all tend to sound the same, they all tend to sound like the author.

They also tend to do things their character wouldn't do. Why? Because the author isn't as interested in who these people are as in what he wants to happen. So the author causes these people to violate their personalities in order to be there when the truck blows up, just so the hero can find motivation to defeat the bad guys.

Not Nobel Prize–level work.

It's hard to do character homework. I know. I get great ideas for story events all the time. But left to what I naturally write, I will create the most shallow, awful, two-dimensional cardboard cutouts that have ever borne the name "characters." I have to work very hard to create characters that are something other than stereotypes.

Still, I hear the call of the road less difficult. How much easier it would be to skip over character work and just get to the explosions. But we must buckle down and do it.

IN PRAISE OF PLOT-FIRST NOVELISTS

Before I let you know the solution to this conundrum, let me talk a moment about how this is a good thing.

If you're a plot-first novelist, rejoice! Your counterparts over there, the novelists who create the most amazing characters since Adam and Eve but couldn't create a plot if their lives depended on it, would give their right arms for the ability to come up with a decent story.

You have a gift, plot writer. Revel in it.

But don't be content with your strengths. Realize that you are incomplete as a craftsman and storyteller. A book with great story elements but lousy characters will end up like *Star Wars: Episode II*, *Jurassic Park: The Lost World*, or *Cliffhanger*. Flashy and even well made but ultimately forgettable.

Until you develop the ability to create interesting and believable characters to populate your novels, your fiction will always be poorer than it could be.

Some plot-first novelists try to solve this by pairing up with a character-first novelist. One writer sets about fashioning terrifically interesting characters, and the other decides what to have them do. If you know someone like this, give co-writing a try.

The best approach, in my opinion, is to *learn to do the thing you're weak at.* Character-first novelists need to learn how to construct interesting plots, and plot-first novelists must learn how to create interesting characters.

A SHAMELESS PITCH

Being a plot-first novelist myself, I tend to think it would be easier for a character-first novelist to learn how to create good plots. All they'd have to do is get the book *20 Master Plots and How to Build Them*, by Ronald Tobias, and start reading and writing.

Personally, I think it's more difficult for the plot-first novelist to learn how to create interesting characters. There are also craft books on how to create great characters for fiction. I own a bunch of them. I recommend you try a few to see if they do the trick for you.

In my own journey I ultimately found these books to be useless for me. I studied them and tried their approaches, but they never worked for me. Part of that is because people who effortlessly create great characters are the ones who write these books. It makes sense: Ask the guy who creates great characters to write a book on creating great characters. But it was as if I wasn't speaking their language.

In the end, I developed my own character creation system, which is available in my Writer's Digest book *Plot Versus Character.*

I've admitted I'm a plot-first novelist who has a hard time coming up with interesting characters who aren't stereotypes and don't all sound like me. So why should you use a character-creation system by a guy like that?

Because I speak your language.

Don't take my word for it; check out my Operation: Firebrand series of novels. With that series I set myself a challenge: Though characters do not come easily to me, could I write a series driven by an ensemble cast?

I didn't want to write *Steel Magnolias,* but I wanted to create a balance between plot-driven and character-driven fiction. If you read one of those novels, and you find yourself thinking fondly of the characters, consider checking out *Plot Versus Character.* If I can create interesting characters as a hardwired plot writer, you can, too.

As long as you commit yourself to creating interesting, believable characters, I (and publishers and readers) will be happy.

For the sake of creating posterity for your fiction, do whatever you must do to create interesting, believable, captivating, and differentiated characters who don't all sound like you.

chapter 11

CREATE A LIKABLE PROTAGONIST

All right, you're convinced of the need to create fully realized characters who don't all sound like you. Excellent. But before we get into the brass tacks of your main character's inner journey and desires, let me just whisper something in your ear: Make sure we like your hero.

Why do you pick up a novel to read? Maybe you like this author or you're in the mood for something in this genre. Maybe you've heard of this book or this writer, and you want to see what all the fuss is about. Maybe you're looking for some pure escapism or an easy summer read. Maybe you just like the cover art.

Underlying your reason for picking up any given novel, whatever the reason, is a set of expectations. You may not even realize you have them.

For one thing, you expect to not be bored. You expect the book to start a certain way and to have certain kinds of characters and situations, according to whatever genre the book is in. You expect the book to be comprehensible. You expect it to entertain you.

You also expect it to have a likable hero.

"I don't have to like the hero," you say. "What about ...?" and you name some story with a protagonist who was a terrorist or a serial killer or an antihero. *Dexter*, a TV show in which the protagonist is a "good" serial killer, comes to mind. So does *Breaking Bad*.

All true. But I contend that while you don't have want to *be like* the protagonist to like the story, in some way you must at least be able to sympathize or empathize with the character. Otherwise you won't keep reading.

Dexter is palatable because he's funny and kills only child predators and the like. He's like a twisted, superhero vigilante.

Jack Sparrow in *Pirates of the Caribbean* is not a particularly nice person. But there's something about him we like. We understand him.

We think he's funny. The ladies think he's cute. We want to see how he's going to get out of any scrape.

Ellen Ripley, Sigourney Weaver's character in the Alien series, is not very pleasant to be around. She's kind of a jerk, actually. But in the first movie she has a cat she's willing to risk her life for. That's something we can understand and sympathize with. In the second movie she's still pretty hard-edged, but she becomes incredibly heroic to save a little girl.

Even Neo in *The Matrix* is not your typical hero. He's a junior slacker at a company, he has authority issues, and he's a drug dealer on the side. But he's got that befuddled look on his face, and the girls think he's cute. And, of course, he helps his landlady carry out her garbage.

Whether we realize it or not, we expect—perhaps even *need*—our protagonists to be likable in some way. Who wants to read about a total jerk?

And yet I regularly see unpublished fiction manuscripts with unlikable heroes. I think these authors are trying to show how awful the person is so that the transition to goodness, when it comes, is more dramatic.

Those are good instincts, but you have to give us a clue early on that there is something good and redeemable in this character, or we'll look elsewhere for entertainment.

This is especially true for stories that have lots of other characters who are unlikable. If your unlikable protagonist is surrounded by awful people doing awful things to each other, and your "hero" is just as awful but gets a starring role, you're going to lose readers in droves.

The movie *Tombstone* is a good example of this. Late in the movie the heroes turn into mass murderers. Whatever moral high ground they had is lost as soon as they become exactly like the bad guys they're up against. Maybe someone somewhere rejoiced in the gritty realism and gray tones of conflicted antiheroes, but to me they became just as despicable as the people they were supposed to be better than. I lost sympathy for the protagonist, an event closely followed by my loss of interest in the movie.

Imagine finding yourself at a party with a bunch of scumbags—and the person who invited you turns out to be the worst of the bunch. You'd excuse yourself from there as quickly as you could.

It works the same in fiction.

THROW US A BONE

There's nothing wrong with conflicted, imperfect protagonists. They are a must. But you have to give your reader some fairly prominent indication right away that this person is heroic, likable, understandable, or at least sympathetic in some way, or your reader will put your book down—simple as that. It's an expectation we have about fiction that we don't consciously realize.

A novel without a likable hero will be a flop even if it has everything else going right. On the other hand, a likable protagonist covers a multitude of fictional sins. A novel can do a lot of things wrong—and take a lot of chances with the story—and get away with it if readers love the hero.

Want to tell a bizarre far-future story about a world in which beings communicate with one another by flapping their appendages in intricate patterns? Give us a likable hero, and we'll stick with your story through any weirdness. Want to tell a dark story that plumbs the depths of man's inhumanity to man? Let us care about your protagonist, and we'll plumb any depth with you.

But give us an irredeemable ogre (with apologies to Shrek) who turns our stomach, and we'll drop your book and move on to something else.

What about the hero in this novel you're planning? Will readers like this person? Or are you trying so hard to be sure your protagonist looks distasteful—to show how far she will come in the course of the novel—that readers can only see black, without a hint of white?

You've got to give at least a glimpse of something that will help your readers consider your protagonist likable. Do it early and do it clearly, and you'll be able to take us on just about any ride you want.

chapter 12
YOUR HERO'S INNER JOURNEY

It is my conviction that 75 percent of your story is your main character's inner journey, or character arc. Now that you know the importance of fully developed characters and of a hero your reader can like, it's time to begin looking at this inner journey.

One thing I often see in new novelists' work is the lack of a satisfying inner journey for their main characters. The protagonist may go through many trials and make a significant decision or take a big risk, but there's something lacking, something organic that would've made the novel truly special.

I believe the best fiction involves a main character who has a problem, issue, or unresolved inner conflict. He's sitting around trying to make it through life but is hindered by this inner problem. He may not even realize he's got this issue. But God knows. And God loves him too much to let him go on this way.

I'm using this terminology intentionally because I believe good fiction represents how God works with mankind. He sees us in our ugliness, with all our deformities, but He also sees our worth, and He extends His love. Even so, the ugliness needs to go. So He starts working on us, forming us into the image of His son.

So it is in fiction. Some people will say that fate is coming in to work on the hero's tragic flaw, and others say it's just the novelist playing God. Whatever works for you. For me, it's God seeing the sin in the person and doing exactly what it takes to bring him to the point where he can choose between the old, sinful way and God's way.

God decides to break out His tools to go to work on this person. He is going to make this character deal with his issue and finally jump off the fence to one side or the other. God is going to force the issue.

In other words, the story is about God helping the protagonist learn a lesson or deal with a problem.

IN A PIT, YOUR LIFE IS ALWAYS LOOKING UP

Most of us must be brought to a place of brokenness before we will accept any kind of major change. Because if it ain't broke, why fix it?

Isn't that how God works with us? He sees the way we sabotage our lives and relationships, and sometimes, because He loves us, He breaks out the power tools to get us fixed. Nobody likes to be drilled, hammered, or cut in two, but that's how the Carpenter builds His masterpieces.

If great fiction is about bringing the main character to a breaking point over a particular "sin," all the events of the story are about bringing the character to that moment. They're God's hammer strokes—or they're the hero's stubborn efforts to resist the change. The more he resists, the more pressure God brings until the hero reaches the breaking point.

I call this the escalating arms race. The more the story tries to cause the hero to change, the more the hero resists, which causes the story to try even harder to get the hero to change.

At rock bottom, when the hero is finally humbled and utterly beaten, he has a choice: surrender to the new way or reject it and go to his doom doing it the old way. When his life is in pieces, and all his old ways have failed him, he's able to begin to "hear" the wisdom of the other way. He's finally willing to give it a try. This is the path that leads to life.

Or he reaches that breaking point and decides he's not going to change no matter what anyone says. He realizes he really is at fault. He acknowledges what has been causing all his problems. But through lust, pride, selfishness, or plain stubbornness, he decides he can't, shouldn't, or won't ever change. And so he pursues a course that leads to his own destruction.

Luke Skywalker, like everyone around him, believes in the prowess of technology. Through the events of *Star Wars: Episode IV* he begins to believe that there is a spiritual power that is greater than technology—whether it's a targeting computer or a Death Star. Flying down the trench in his X-wing, he reaches his point of decision—to which the whole story has been driving—and he makes his choice.

Lightning McQueen thinks he's the only character of importance in *Cars*. He offends and walks on people and as a result has no friends. The "accidental" detour to Radiator Springs eventually forces him to care for a community. In the big Piston Cup race at the end, he has the choice to apply the lesson the story has been teaching him—that he needs others to be complete—or to reject the lesson and go back to his old ways.

Getting the character to that breaking point is what the whole story has been about. What he decides in that moment of truth spells his salvation or his damnation.

This is the story of man. We can't live without God, though we try to. God comes to us in mercy and pushes us to the end of ourselves, urging us to surrender and accept God's way. Either we do or we don't. But our eternity hangs in the balance as we choose.

LAND THIS PLANE, MISTER

What about your story? What is the issue or flaw your protagonist has? What is her "knot" that must be untied? What does God want to teach her? How will God use the story to bring her to a point of accepting or rejecting that change? How will the protagonist work to resist making that change? What does rock bottom look like for the character in this story? What will she ultimately decide?

This is your protagonist's inner journey, her character arc. It is a journey with an observable and predictable trajectory. Include this in your fiction, and it will feel well rounded and spiritually complete. Ignore it, and readers (and editors) will feel that there is a certain ineffable *something* missing from your novel.

chapter 13

WHEN DO PEOPLE CHANGE?

As we've just seen, the crux of great fiction is bringing your protagonist to the moment when he is willing to consider two paths—the old way and the new way—and make the choice. The whole story is about getting the character to that moment of truth.

But what causes people to willingly contemplate change? This chapter is all about that crucial escalating arms race that leads your protagonist to the moment when the choice is made and all of heaven holds its breath.

FORMULA ONE

I'm not a fan of formula fiction. But sometimes there are formulas you can use to help your fiction. I don't mean a mathematical formula for determining page count based on word count or something like that. I mean theoretical formulas that can help you as you're writing.

Here's a good one for when you're contemplating your character's inner journey: People don't change until the cost of staying the same gets too high.

Think about someone who doesn't want to flee a potentially dangerous flood.

> He stays home when others pack up and leave. When the TV says everyone should leave, he stays. When the police come by and tell him to leave, he stays. When the water begins to rise, he stays. He gets an ice chest of Buds and sits in a lawn chair on the roof, his shotgun across his knees.
>
> No one's getting his stuff. Besides, the flood won't do what those college boys on TV keep saying, he thinks to himself. What do they know about these woods?

> But then the water keeps rising. Cars flood. Bloated animal corpses float by in the current. The only signs of human life are news helicopters, National Guard choppers, and the occasional passing inflatable boat carrying a family and their belongings.

Now our man's getting worried.

> Was this such a good idea? No one's going to steal his stuff. Indeed, the water's already entered the first floor and ruined or carried off most of it. If things keep going like they're headed, he's going to lose more than his collection of Johnny Cash CDs and his mama's prize-winning quilts.
>
> The water keeps rising. It's crashed through the second-story windows now. The house is a total loss. Worse, there haven't been any helicopters in the last three hours.
>
> What's that upstream in the brown water? Something big: a flotilla of debris being pushed along in front of it as by the blade of a bulldozer. One end of it bobs in the dirty rapids, and he catches a glimpse of what is: the pier from Jacobs' Marina five miles upstream.
>
> It's headed right toward his house, broadside, like a giant eraser about to wipe his homestead from its foundation.
>
> The nearly submerged pier strikes the oak tree where he played as a child. The ancient tree resists at first. The pier stalls, and the floodwaters rise angrily behind it. But then the oak gives way, victim to a force of nature. The pier surges forward, rotating in the water toward his house like a three-ton torpedo.
>
> Now he wants to leave. Now, finally, he's ready to change.
>
> All his resolve is gone. He's going to die. And for what? Forget it. Nothing is worth this. Why, oh, why hadn't he left when he could?
>
> The pier is thirty feet away and coming fast. He drops his shotgun, kicks off his boots, and leaps into the frigid water, using his empty ice chest as a flotation device.

When did our man make a change? When his life was in danger. Until that point he was willing to stay and fend off the change, even though everyone else had changed before then. He resisted. In his mind, the cost of changing was too great, and so he stayed the same. Heroic.

SO SHOULD YOUR CHARACTERS

As we've seen, I believe the best fiction is about people who must change but don't want to. The events of the story come along to force change, but they resist. They've found something that's working for them, or so they think, and the pain of changing is too great. So they refuse.

But the events of the story change the picture. They bring about an escalation that begins to even out the pros and cons. For most of the story it's still too costly for the character to change, so he fights to keep things the way they were, even escalating his own desperate attempts to maintain the status quo.

Finally the cost becomes too great. The story (or God or fate) provides the last straw, breaking our character's resolve. He is broken, defeated. Finally he realizes that staying the same will cause more damage than changing. The floodwaters of the story have risen to the point that it's no longer worth it to stick to the old ways.

And so he jumps. Or, if you're writing a tragic inner journey for him, he lashes himself to the chimney and goes down with the house.

But the whole story is about getting him to that moment of choice. That's the stuff of true drama.

Think of Lieutenant Dan in *Forrest Gump*. He was angry with God because of what had happened to him in Vietnam. The two of them had a grudge match going on, at least from Lieutenant Dan's perspective. And God kept throwing hardships at him until that climactic scene when *Jenny* is in dire straits, and Dan goes overboard, screaming at God.

Through that moment he is broken and he finds his peace with God. But if God hadn't brought the hardships and the storm, Dan would've remained trapped in his self-destructive anger and depression.

People do not change until the cost of staying the same is greater than the cost of changing.

So how do you want that to happen in your story? Your job as a novelist is to raise the stakes, increase the cost, and bring the floodwaters. Your character is stuck in his ways. He's happy with this situation, even though it is a problem. It's destroying him. He doesn't see it or won't admit it. But it's better than the alternative. Changing would hurt too much.

You have to make it hurt too much for him to stay the same.

When he finally gets to the point where he realizes he really would be better off if he changed, but he still has strong reasons to cling to the old way—and he knows he must choose or perish—your reader will watch breathlessly to see what he decides.

And that, my friend, is a good thing.

As you evaluate your story and your characters' inner journeys, call up this formula to be sure you're getting the balance right.

chapter 14
WHAT DOES YOUR HERO WANT?

By this point in "Focus on the Craft: Character," you have probably thought a bit about what your protagonist wants. For one thing, she wants to avoid the painful change God is bringing upon her.

But that's in her inner journey. There should be something else she wants in her external journey. It should relate to the inner journey on some level, even if she doesn't realize it. But as far as she's concerned, it's a logical goal with nothing more to it than what appears on the surface. So what does she want to achieve—or prevent—in your story?

Luke Skywalker wants to defeat the Empire. If he doesn't, freedom in the galaxy will perish. Lightning McQueen wants to get out of Radiator Springs to get to California for the Piston Cup. If he doesn't, his dream to win the cup as a rookie will die. E.T. wants to get home. If he doesn't, he'll be stranded on Earth forever, where he's dying. Frodo wants to get to the Cracks of Mount Doom and throw the Ring in to destroy it. If he doesn't, all the free peoples of Middle-earth will be enslaved.

In simplest terms, a novel is about a hero who wants something and the consequences if she doesn't get it.

I'm surprised at how many aspiring novelists lose sight of this and write meandering stories that seem to lose their way, leaving readers adrift.

No matter what happens to your protagonist, you can't have her forget what she was originally after. She may realize, of course, that what she *needed* was something else, but it has to resonate with the reader.

In *Cars*, Lightning McQueen thought what he wanted was to get to California to win the race. But he discovered he needed to learn humility and an appreciation for others around him. He still gets to his race, but by then his heart has changed.

Luke Skywalker realized he needed to align himself with the Force and to later redeem his father. He still opposed the Empire, but his goals became more focused.

What about your story? Do you have your hero wanting more than anything to pass a bill in the Senate, and halfway through you have her caring more about deep-sea fishing? Was your hero originally trying to mend his marriage, but the climax is about the recovery of a stolen artifact? Don't let your hero forget what he's after.

In your story, you'll need to decide: Who is your hero? Are you *sure* you know? What does your hero want? What stands in the way of your hero getting what he wants? How is he pursuing that goal in every scene? What are the stakes? What will happen if the hero doesn't get what he wants?

Will the hero's goal become more focused as the story progresses? If so, how and why? Does this "redirected" goal make sense with what he thought he wanted at the outset? Will your hero attain his goal?

When you answer these questions, your protagonist's goals will be clear to the reader, which will keep the story pointed in the right direction.

chapter 15

HOW TO BRING YOUR MAIN CHARACTER ONSTAGE

All right, now we're getting to the part of character creation that transitions to writing the book.

AND NOW I AM PLEASED TO INTRODUCE ...

Many novelists give little thought to how they bring their protagonist onstage for the first time. But this is very important.

It establishes the character and what she is about in the reader's mind. These things are vital for your hero, your antagonist, and possibly a handful of supporting characters as well.

Remember the opening sequence in *Raiders of the Lost Ark*—that scene in the jungle where Indy is going after the golden idol? By the time that series of scenes is completed, our hero is flying away in a water plane, and we know a lot about our main character.

We know he's an American who goes on international treasure hunts. We know he's tough, savvy, and fearless; he uses a whip and is fond of his fedora; he knows his way around ancient ruins. We also know his chief adversary. Finally, we learn his ultimate fear: snakes.

When that sequence is over, we feel like we know our hero *and* we've learned what kind of movie this is going to be. It's a masterful introduction of the story's protagonist (and villain).

You should do this with your hero, too.

Now, you don't have to take much page space to introduce your hero in your novel. That sequence ran about twenty minutes, roughly one-sixth of the movie. Spending one-sixth of your novel introducing your protagonist is overkill.

What I want you to take away from this example is that the storyteller was consciously introducing his protagonist so all the things we need to know about him are presented to the audience.

What is your protagonist's essential characteristic? Do you know? At this point in the character-creation process, I hope you know it well. What is it that makes him heroic and likable? Because, as we saw in Chapter 11, if the reader doesn't like your hero, you're doomed before you begin.

With this essential quality in mind, begin thinking about how you could illustrate your characteristic in action. What would be an ideal way to *show* your hero doing something that reveals this essential characteristic? Think of a scene that introduces your story's world, is consistent with the tone of your entire story, and shows us exactly who this character is.

That's how to introduce your protagonist.

A HINT OF TROUBLE

In the introductory scene include a hint about what's wrong with your protagonist. What is the knot or problem his inner journey will be about? Do you have something wrong or unresolved going on with him? Your protagonist must have a satisfying inner journey, which means he must begin the story in a flawed condition. That flaw ought to come out at some point during the scene in which he first steps onstage, even if it's only barely glimpsed.

The first time we see your protagonist we should see: (1) what's likable/heroic about her, (2) what her essential characteristic is, and (3) what weakness or incompleteness your story is going to address in her inner journey.

Be conscious of how you introduce your villain, too. Develop a scene that reveals his character and illustrates what is villainous about him. What is *his* essential characteristic? How could you show that?

Your important supporting characters, such as romantic interests and sidekicks, should be brought onstage in a carefully crafted way, too.

Don't forget these introductory scenes all still need to advance your story. You can't stop your narrative just to have a song and dance to bring on a new character. Every scene has to do double- or triple-duty: introducing a character, advancing the plot, and establishing a location that will be important later, for example.

If you've taken the time to fully craft your characters, coming up with the ideal way to bring each one of them onstage ought to be a breeze for you.

Design the opening scene for your main characters with all the care you'd bring if each one were a short story. You'll reap the benefits later on if you have introduced your main characters correctly. Keep the example from *Raiders of the Lost Ark* in mind. And bring those characters onstage with careful thought.

chapter 16
DIFFERENTIATING MULTIPLE, SIMILAR CHARACTERS

If you stay in the fiction game long enough, you'll eventually want to write a story in which several characters are superficially similar to one another. Whether it's a water-polo team, a widows' Sunday school class, or the crew of a pirate ship, you'll be faced with the challenge of making virtually identical characters distinct in the minds of your readers.

It can certainly be done, but it's a path that plot-first novelists should fear to tread. If the characters you tend to write aren't known for their distinctiveness (or even if they are), you'll need to work extra hard to make sure the reader can tell the players apart without a program.

THE CHALLENGE

Few challenges in fiction are as vexing as writing stories that feature a group of characters who are all basically the same: age, gender, race, occupation, location, and situation in life. Think about a football team, a cheerleading squad, or an army platoon.

Now, if you're just writing the group at a distance, you're usually okay. If, for instance, the women's fast-pitch softball team simply passes the protagonist in an airport, there's no need to single out more than one or two from the group, if any.

But if you're going to zoom in and spend time with these characters, you're in for a challenge.

Some writers plunge right in, unaware of the difficulties. I see this a lot among male writers or anyone who could be classified as a plot-first novelist. These writers seem inordinately drawn to this kind of story, whether it's the fantasy army, the B-17 crew, or the basketball team.

Their fiction is usually characterized by dozens of characters who all seem identical to the reader. Wait, is Hopkins the one with the glasses or the one from Philly? Everything is apparently straight in the author's mind, but the reader can't tell Jenkins from Johnson and Johnson from Jones.

As an editor, I sometimes see manuscripts in which words that had been said by one character in a previous version are now said by another character, and the story isn't affected one bit.

That's a clue for you: If you're able to just change the name tags of your characters, and nothing seems wrong afterward, something needs to be fixed.

Here's an area where movies have it much easier than novels. All you have to do in a movie is cast two actors and point the camera at them: The viewer can see the difference for herself. Got ten guys in a squad? Just cast ten actors who don't all look the same, and you're golden. In novels, readers don't have the luxury of a constant reinforcement and differentiation between otherwise similar characters.

WHAT'S A BODY TO DO?

I asked several of my published Christian novelist friends how they handle writing about groups of similar characters. Here are some of their ideas.

You can *create a reporter or investigator* character who travels with the group. This person has a built-in reason to interview and study (and describe for the reader) each character in your group. This trick makes the reader somewhat more tolerant of exposition, because the in-depth description is part of the character's job. It has the side effect of getting us more than skin deep with your characters. It's a good application of my famous "dumb-puppet trick" (which we'll talk about in Part III).

Another way to meet this challenge is to *concentrate on physical differences* between the similar characters. It's true that ten soldiers standing in a line might seem identical to the casual observer, but a mother would be able to pick out her son almost instantly. Each character will have a distinctive coloring, build, nose size, eye color, hair texture, beard or shadow thickness, hand size, lip color, haircut, tattoos or scars, complexion, head size, face shape, posture, and more.

I think this is a good one. You can and should use obvious physical differences to help readers tell characters apart. But remember, unless you're constantly reminding readers about these differences, they won't be able to keep track of them. It might become a little comic: big-nose talks to no-earlobe while playing cards with pimple-face.

Another idea my fellow novelists came up with is to *group some of the similar characters together* in twos or threes. Remember Samneric in *Lord of the Flies*? They were really twin brothers Sam and Eric, but they were always together and even finished one another's sentences. It was as if they were one person: two characters for the price of one.

Perhaps you can do that with some of the characters in your group. One book I worked on had "the Irishmen" together in a machine gun team. These were three guys who didn't need to be differentiated beyond that designation for the purposes of the story.

However, when we start saying that certain groups of people don't need to be well defined, we need to be careful. As soon as a novelist thinks it's okay to leave certain characters as caricatures, he's probably stepping into the realm of plot-first writing, which can leave many characters shallow. This in turn leaves that novelist's fiction unpublishable. But the further from the reader's attention the characters are, the safer it is to clump them together for convenience.

You can *use rank or status distinctions.* If you're writing about a military team, there will be a variety of ranks within the group. These can help differentiate your characters. But even if your team isn't military, there will be variations in tasks, roles, and leadership positions within the group. There are bosses and flunkies, freelancers and lifers, the new kid and the office floozy. A volleyball team has a team captain, the starters, the hitters, the setters, the back-row specialists, the blockers, and the jump servers. Not to mention the coach, equipment boy, team trainers, etc.

Rank and status differences can help you make distinctions and find subgroups within the larger group. You'll need all the tools at your disposal, trust me.

Another idea is to *use nicknames* for your characters. You've got Gunny, Cookie, Sarge, and LT. Why not make up creative nicknames for your characters?

Speaking of volleyball, many years ago I went to a volleyball tournament with a team of older guys who needed a sixth player for the weekend. The team's organizer was a guy who didn't seem to feel the need to learn anyone's name. He preferred to make up nicknames. It was hysterical, really, and revealed a lot about his character. Maybe he had trouble with his memory so he made things easier by using nicknames. Maybe he felt out of control in his life and compensated by renaming everyone and categorizing them according to his preferences. So we all had nicknames, things like Red, Slick, Junior, Hippie, and Grandpa. I think the team captain was the only one allowed to go by his real name.

It worked for him, and it might work for you, too, especially if your viewpoint character is the one assigning the nicknames.

A variation of this is to let the viewpoint character "tag" people with de facto nicknames.

> Clarice went to a party in which Hair Lady was stuck talking to Loud Guy. Dixie and Trixie were babbling on about makeup, and sitting alone in the corner was Sad Guy, thinking about nihilism.

So long as you're not spending too much time with these characters, such appellations are fine and can help characterize your viewpoint character.

You can *use a prop or a habit* to help differentiate characters. Maybe one girl is always eating gummy bears. Maybe another always carries a romance novel under her arm. Another might constantly twirl her hair. Another might smell of garlic. Another might always wear something fuchsia.

In theater, many beginning actors like to have props. It gives them something to do with their hands. From a fiction perspective, a prop or habit gives the novelist some built-in ways to help remind the reader who this character is.

Remember Edward James Olmos's character in *Blade Runner*? He was a creepy detective guy named Gaff. He always folded little origami creatures. There's a key moment late in the film when we don't know who did something, but there's a little origami unicorn on the floor, and we know who it was. Consider giving your characters a prop or distinctive habit.

These are all very good ideas, and you should use one or more of them if you're writing a story with many similar characters. But let's turn to what I think is the best way to differentiate multiple characters who are otherwise indistinguishable to the reader.

FIRST, DO NO HARM

As I said before, filmmakers have it easy when differentiating between multiple, similar characters. All they have to do is point the camera at them, and the viewer has constant reinforcement about who is who. However, even in film and TV this is sometimes difficult.

There are two women in *The Lake House* who seem identical to me, even after multiple viewings. (The actresses are Shohreh Aghdashloo and Willeke van Ammelrooy.) I think the casting director made a mistake to cast them both in the same film, especially since they're both in motherly roles for our heroine.

There's a reason actors are cast not only for their acting abilities but also for how they look beside the rest of the cast. In a show like *Band of Brothers* you have to do all you can to make sure the guys look different.

If it's difficult to tell these people apart in a movie, what's a novelist to do?

The first thing to do is to not put yourself in this situation in the first place, if you can avoid it. Try to cast a woman in a group that you had originally envisioned as a trio of men. Cast a child, a very old man, or someone of a different race. Do what you can to avoid scenarios where you have multiple people the reader will have trouble telling apart.

But sometimes the story you choose will force you to have similar people together in the story. If that's the case, you must know your characters inside and out.

NOVELIST, KNOW THY CHARACTERS

I consider weak characters to be one of the three marks of bad fiction (along with telling and POV errors). Whether characters come naturally to you or not, you must do your homework to create realistic characters. If this is true for a normal novel, how much more accurate is it for a character-driven novel and an ensemble cast?

If you don't utterly know your characters, the reader won't have a prayer.

There's a saying in preaching: "If it's a haze in the pulpit, it's a fog in the pew." In other words, if the preacher doesn't have it straight, the audience will be entirely confused. The same goes for writers and their audience.

If you don't know (or care) who the people are in your story, the reader certainly won't. When it comes to writing a story with several similar characters, you must know your characters extremely well, even better than in a "regular" story that isn't so confusing.

Plot-first novelists tend to gravitate to this kind of story, which can be a problem, because they generally don't care about their characters (not as compared to the story, anyway). For these novelists, characters are merely there to die and provide the hero a justification to get vengeance, thus propelling the plot.

So it's already like pulling teeth to get these writers to do any homework on their characters. And then to tell them that they have to do that level of work for each of the *similar* characters in their book … Many of them would just rather not.

Which is fine. No problem. But if they skip this work, they can't complain when reviewers say all their characters seem the same.

I know you're willing to do the hard work of creating good characters, or you wouldn't still be reading this.

The secret is doing your character homework. You need to know your characters well to pull this off. When you do, the differences between characters will become apparent to the reader. Not immediately, perhaps, but eventually. If you've got their personalities distinct in *your* mind, the differences will come out on the page.

So be tolerant of a few pages of similarity before the characters' distinctive personalities emerge for the reader. You don't necessarily have to make them perfectly distinctive the first time they're onstage. But an introduction that distinguishes them would be nice.

Just as you would eventually learn to know the difference between twin sisters, so the reader will eventually learn to tell the difference between multiple characters who seem otherwise the same—so long as they really do have distinctive personalities.

HOW SHE SAID IT

You can usually distinguish between characters in a movie just by looking at them. But in a novel, saying a character is present in a scene doesn't have the same power to remind the reader of who that character is as a camera has in a movie. Every frame of film reinforces that character's persona. Not so with every line in a novel. Readers can forget who characters are, especially when they're very similar.

So what's the novelist to do? You know your characters now, so you're sure the difference will manifest itself eventually. But if only you could have at your disposal something akin to the filmmaker's constant reminder.

Guess what? You do! It's called *dialogue.*

We'll cover dialogue in depth in a "Focus on the Craft" section, but this is a good place to introduce it because it's an outgrowth of character. *How the character speaks* is the novelist's means of always keeping that character's distinctiveness before the reader's eyes.

What he says, how he says it, what he talks about, the presence or absence of humor, his level of diction, his vocabulary choice, his mastery of English, the use of parenthetical phrases, and the presence or absence of word pictures, malapropisms, and regional colloquialisms all help build the gestalt of any person's distinctive way of speaking.

The manner in which a person speaks—and what she chooses to speak about and when—is the best way of revealing who that person is. It reveals her personality, interests, education, and even intelligence. It exposes what she cares about, what agendas she's pursuing, and what she's afraid of. How a character speaks reveals who she is.

So put on Henry Higgins's tweed hat and examine how "an Englishman's way of speaking absolutely classifies him." As soon as a character opens his mouth in your novel, it ought to be (or become) clear to the reader who is speaking.

Wouldn't that be awesome? As soon as the character makes a peep, the reader knows who it is. Even without any other description.

When my daughter was reading *Harry Potter and the Order of the Phoenix*, she told me all a certain character had to do was cough in a particular way and she knew instantly the villain was in the scene. J.K.

Rowling could write one word—or one sound—and the reader knew which character it was. That's great character work.

The manner of a person's speaking is the window to his soul, as perhaps Jesus meant when He said that what proceeds out of a person's mouth is the truest glimpse into his heart (Matthew 15:11).

The way a character speaks is to your fiction what a camera shot of the character speaking is to cinema. This doesn't mean you should concentrate on making your characters sound distinctive. Don't give them all crazy accents or speech impediments. That's a lazy shortcut. The end result of great character work is every character reveals his distinctiveness simply by opening his mouth. But trying to jump to the end and just distinguish your characters by having one surfer dude, one Oxford graduate, one Indian immigrant, and one Fonzie clone is not going to have the same result. You'll have even worse caricatures than you had before.

Please commit yourself to doing this the right way. Take the time to know your characters. We're all about trying to bring to God a sacrifice of excellence, remember? Say with King David that you will bring no sacrifice to God that cost you nothing (1 Chronicles 21:24).

Differentiating multiple, similar characters goes back to old-fashioned character development work. You can and should make use of all the techniques listed by my peers, you can try to avoid these situations in the first place, and you can try other ideas. Bring new characters in ones and twos, as opposed to all at once, in order to give your reader a handle on some characters before being asked to learn all of them.

But in the end, the best way to be sure your reader can differentiate between multiple characters, who are otherwise similar is to know your characters so well you can tell who is who simply by their dialogue.

chapter 17
CHARACTERS SERVING PLOT

We come now to the final portion of our first "Focus on the Craft" section. By now you should be deeply into the development of your terrific, unforgettable characters. The last strategic element of character creation is to be sure your characters propel the plot, not serve it.

For example: The woman who has been terrified of being attacked by a monster during the course of the story suddenly decides to let the rest of the group go on ahead so she can be left alone in the creepy deserted mansion to catch her breath. Yeah, right.

The scientist whose only concern in life is to keep a natural environment free of all signs of human impact tears off a candy wrapper and throws it in the grass. Oh, really?

The expert chess player makes an erroneous comment about the rules of chess and thereby reveals that he is really the killer. Sure.

Why would a novelist make characters do such things? Because the novelist needed something to happen in the plot and didn't mind violating who these characters were, so long as the plot advanced.

This is called "character serving plot," and you should strive to never, ever do it.

The author wanted the woman to be alone when the monster attacked, so he made the character do something she would never do. The novelist needed the audience to dislike the scientist, so he caused the scientist to violate the essence of his character. The author needed the detective to break the case at this moment, so he caused the character to do something he would never do and give himself away.

Character serving plot is among the most atrocious sins of fiction. The novelist who does this, who violates her characters' personalities and patterns so the plot can be advanced, insults her readers' intelligence.

Allegedly the reader won't notice that this character is supposed to be a computer expert but conveniently forgets how to check e-mail. The reader won't be bothered if a songwriter doesn't notice when one of his own songs is being played on the radio. And the reader won't think it odd that a detective with thirty years' experience doesn't notice when three cars and a helicopter are following him.

Now, I love plot-first novelists. I am one. But, bless us, we tend to move characters around the story like the race car and the shoe in Monopoly. Characters are things to us, like furniture or pets.

In our furniture-moving and pet-herding, plot-first novelists can sometimes make characters do things they wouldn't naturally do. That's because they (the writers) don't know who their characters are, actually. With most of them you could change the character names all around, and no one would be able to tell the difference.

> "That sounds good," Mike said.
>
> "Yeah, I love it," Steve said.

... becomes ...

> "That sounds good," Lorraine said.
>
> "Yeah, I love it," Betty said.

And you can't tell the difference—all the way through the book.

If you're a plot-first novelist, and I hope you know whether you are or not, I beg you to get to know your characters better. Make them more than the thing that gets blown up to make the hero mad and go on a revenge killing spree, okay?

When you know your characters, it will suddenly feel wrong when your professional singer doesn't know how to read music or when you make your Olympic figure skater a real klutz.

You may not be able to see if you're doing this. This might be one of those things where you need someone else to read your manuscript and tell you when you're having characters serve plot. If so, get someone to do that for you. Ask someone to read it looking for that thing only, especially if you know you're prone to this. Better yet, get it fixed before you even start writing. Do it while you're still strategizing.

Begin treating your characters like real people, not chess pieces. Begin liking them as unique individuals, not stereotypes from the movies. Do that and you will learn how to let characters be themselves and do the things they would truly do.

When that happens, you'll have to figure out another way for the dinosaurs to eat them or the detective to figure out they're the killer. But I have no doubt you'll be able to do that. Just be sure you don't violate some other character's traits when you come up with your solution.

Let characters act like they really would act if they were real, and your readers will rise up and call you blessed.

chapter 18
THE TICKING TIME BOMB

Now that you've strategized yourself as a novelist, found your story, and done all that terrific work to know and introduce your characters, only a few strategic matters remain before we turn to actually writing your novel.

It may feel like a lot of work to do before you get started, but just like making sure you come to the work site with all the tools you'll need, doing these things first will become something you're deeply thankful for later.

DO YOU HEAR THAT TICKING?

At some point, every novelist hates his book and wants to blow it up. Verily, verily, I say unto you, you will eventually summon the Holy Hand Grenade of Antioch.

But that's not what I'm talking about here.

Here I'm talking about suspense. I'm talking about giving your novel an overriding sense of urgency that increases the tension with every chapter and scene that passes.

The easiest illustration of this is a literal ticking time bomb. Think of the movie *Speed*. The bomb was ticking, the bus was running out of gas, and the villain was about to get his wish of blowing up the passengers. How long could our heroine keep the bus moving above the minimum speed? She was getting tired. It was nerve-wracking and wonderful. Audiences were gripped, and every second that passed ratcheted up the suspense even further.

All because of a ticking time bomb.

Now what about something just as dramatic, like an impending volcanic eruption (*Dante's Peak*) or an asteroid on a collision course for Earth (*Armageddon*)? Every moment that passes brings disaster closer. Our heroes, of course, are right in harm's way. Thanks to these built-in suspense-creating devices, the storyteller had ever-increasing suspense working to the benefit of the story.

YOU, TOO, CAN BE A MAD BOMBER

You don't have to write screenplays for Hollywood blockbusters to harness the power of the ticking time bomb. Why not put something like this in your story? As you strategically contemplate your book, now is the best time to think about this.

It doesn't have to be as large or dramatic as an Earth-destroying asteroid, though. Any impending event that will be bad for the hero if it's not prevented is a candidate for a ticking time bomb.

If the hero doesn't raise the money by the end of the month, the bank is going to repossess the house. If the hero can't learn this material for the test at the end of the week, she'll be kicked out of school and have to move away from her boyfriend. If the kids don't find the way out of the sewers before the scheduled release of the dam's floodgates, they'll drown.

Every novel needs stakes. (And stakes are what we're talking about here.) Every novel needs suspense of some kind to propel the story forward and to impel the reader to keep reading. If there's nothing at risk and nothing in jeopardy, what's the point? If everyone is sitting around well fed, taken care of, and in no danger of losing anything or failing to achieve something, how boring would that be?

When we lived in Orlando, we weathered three direct-hit hurricanes in one season. On the day of the first one, all we could do was watch the radar sweeps and feel the wind increasing outside. Every one of those brightly colored radar sweeps (which updated only every five minutes—another great suspense technique) showed that this massive swirling vortex of death had moved a tiny bit closer to our house.

It was excruciating. Talk about mounting suspense. My poor daughter, in elementary school then, was getting increasingly anxious. The hurricane was a fast mover, but still it took all day and into the night to arrive.

Finally it hit. It was pitch dark outside (just to add to the feeling of claustrophobia), and we were all strung out with stress. Around midnight my daughter was wide awake but stretched tight. I happened to be on the phone with my brother-in-law in Texas, who was concerned because he knew the eye of the storm was going to pass right over our house. Suddenly a giant gust of wind hit us, and the lights went out with a *clack*.

My daughter let loose with the scream heard 'round the world—or at least all the way from Florida to Texas.

That's the cumulative power of the ticking time bomb. It makes the reader worry about it for a long time, and when it finally arrives, suspense is at a fever pitch.

You should consider using such a device, too. Find some dire eventuality that the hero doesn't want to happen and put it in your story. Let its shadow loom over his path for the whole book. Make it something that can be announced early in the story (to begin the countdown for the reader), arrive at the climax, and you'll raise the suspense throughout your novel.

One last note about the ticking time bomb: The hero doesn't necessarily need to know anything about it. The main thing is that the *reader* knows about it. Sometimes it's even more effective for the reader to know that a disaster is coming but for the characters not to know. Play with different options, but definitely consider setting the explosives and getting them ticking.

chapter 19

THE *DEUS EX MACHINA*

As you think strategically about your story, there are three no-nos of Christian fiction to avoid. By making sure you are aware of them before your story has begun, you'll be better able to steer clear of these areas when you're writing. The first of these no-nos is the *deus ex machina*.

GOD FROM THE MACHINE

In Greek theater, tragedies especially, the human characters made a royal mess of things. And then, when it looked like there was simply no solution to it all, a god would appear and sort everything out. "You marry her; you say you're sorry. You, you have to die—sorry." Zap.

This has come to be known as the *deus ex machina* (literally: god from the machine) because of the mechanical crane that was used to lower the actor who played the god so he could bring about a resolution to the story. Today we say a novel has a *deus ex machina* ending if something comes in and magically fixes everything back to the way it should be.

Such a literary device worked in ancient Greece, but I hope you can see how it's really a cop-out. It's too convenient, and it doesn't arise from the story. Christian novelists, who are used to dealing with the supernatural all day long, are especially prone to writing an ending like this.

Let's say you're writing a Western. You've got the bad guys surrounding the good guys, outnumbering them a hundred to one. The pretty schoolmarm is in the clutches of the antagonist, and the stampede is coming. The hero is tied to the train tracks, and the locomotive is bearing down. There's really no good ending here (for the good guys).

But instead of letting the bad guys win for once or showing the hero's ingenious escape to save the day, you bring in an angel. Suddenly a bright light appears, and the cattle stop in their tracks. The angel points, and a lightning bolt melts the locomotive's engine, stopping it. She zaps the archvillain and levitates the schoolmarm into the hero's (magically untied) arms. She sweeps her angelic wings, and all the villains are turned to dust. Huzzah.

As readers, we're certainly glad things worked out the way we wanted, but this ending doesn't feel exactly right. This ending feels like cheating. The resolution we were hoping for happened, but no one in the story did anything to bring it about. If the angel was going to do all that, why didn't she just do it at the outset and save the characters from running around?

The reader feels cheated. The ending feels too convenient and random. Even if the bad guys had won, at least the story would've ended in a logical way.

Your ending has to arise from your beginning. It has to make sense and be organic to the story as you've presented it. The best endings feel inevitable; they feel *right* to the reader. A surprise ending, in which some outside force comes in and makes everything work out correctly, feels wrong to the reader.

Most novelists know to avoid the *deus ex machina* ending. They abide by the old adage: "Don't let good luck or the Good Lord save your hero." Most novelists don't go there. But *Christian novelists* are especially vulnerable to using it, all the same.

We're all about writing stories that include a spiritual component, right? So why not use that component at the climax of our stories? Didn't the characters pray? Don't we want to tell readers that prayer works? What could illustrate that better than having God show up and do something miraculous at the climax of the story?

The problem is that this is still a cheesy ending. It's still God from the machine—inorganic resolution to your story. It's also not an accurate portrayal of the Christian life.

You must figure out a way for your hero, perhaps using divine guidance received earlier in the story, to pull off the victory. Don't let God save the day by direct intervention.

YEAH, BUT ...

There are some exceptions. When your story is expressly *about* the power of God, then sometimes seeing that power displayed is, in fact, the most organic resolution to your story.

For instance, in my sixth novel, *Operation: Firebrand—Deliverance*, I tell a story about God's intervention. One character is questioning God's existence. He's heard that God is working among a fiercely persecuted people (North Koreans), and he feels he needs to see something like that himself. He's a doubting Thomas.

All along in the story there are strange and possibly miraculous goings-on. There have been reports of titanic warriors appearing and aiding the oppressed as they flee for safety. But our American characters have not seen any of this.

The climax of this story has this character doing something stupidly heroic, thinking he will die in the process—mainly because he has concluded that God won't intervene.

During that action sequence, mysterious warriors appear and help him escape. He thinks it's his own team come to bail him out, but when he gets away he encounters his own team at the rendezvous point. Who were those guys back there?

It ends up being the answer to his question about faith. Even though he is unsuccessful in what he was trying to do, he realizes now there is something to God's supernatural power. I believe God sometimes meets us right where we are and gives us exactly what we need, even though most of the time it seems He wouldn't do so.

Technically, that story's climax uses a *deus ex machina*. Something besides human intervention helped our hero escape. But because the point of the whole story had been about God's power and intervention, I felt it was justified. Indeed, to not have it would've been a wrong ending, in my opinion.

You just have to be cautious about using such an ending. Almost always err on the side of not using a divine-intervention ending.

LET THE ENDING ARISE FROM THE BEGINNING

The way your story resolves must organically arise from how the story began. Here's another way of saying it: Your ending must be built into your beginning.

I can't tell you how many unpublished novels I've read in which the ending has absolutely nothing to do with the beginning.

For two hundred pages we've been dealing with this guy's decision of whether or not to euthanize his elderly mother who has been in a coma for twenty years, but the ending is about him foiling a bank robbery. Or for three hundred pages we've been following this woman's story to free a group of prisoners, but the ending is a courtroom drama in which the hero proves that a law about building codes should be illegal.

This is an example of something I call plant and payoff. In Part III I'll talk about these concepts, but here's a preview. You have to establish something before you can use it, and if you establish something, you must do something with it. This principle applies to how you begin and end your story. How you begin your novel establishes what your story is going to be about. Your poor reader comes to expect that the ending of the story is going to be about the very thing your story began with.

I know some novelists like to just launch into a story with no clue about where it's heading. That's cool with me. Even those writers who use detailed outlines do include some spontaneity when they have a better idea while writing.

So maybe you shouldn't worry about the ending as you're writing. Maybe you just write the thing and see where you end up. That's fine.

Just be sure to go back and fix the beginning. That's why we're talking about this now, in the strategic section. Once you've found your story and discovered where it's going, you can go back and rewrite your beginning so the reader will be able to see (in retrospect only, perhaps) that the seeds of the book's resolution were perceptible in the beginning.

If you write a novel that is largely based on the protagonist's inner journey, this will be no problem for you. You've written an introductory scene for your character that shows, among other things, his knot or problem. (You have, right?)

Then the whole book is about him coming to grips with that problem. And *then* the story's climax is his moment of truth in which he'll decide how he's going to deal with that problem. Just by nature of including a good character arc, you will have ensured your ending is planted in the beginning.

Your story's ending must have grown organically from how it began and developed along the way. Do that and you're well on your way to making sure your reader is satisfied with your story.

The antidote to a *deus ex machina* story is one in which the ending grows organically from the beginning and doesn't involve an outside force magically fixing everything. Build it in from the outset.

chapter 20
A SERMON IN THE MIDDLE OF THE STORY

The second no-no in Christian fiction is the book that hinges on a sermon (or equivalent) that tells the hero what to do to fix the problem.

I don't know whether to call this a form of telling, a fiction cliché, agenda-driven fiction, *deus ex machina*, or just a personal pet peeve of mine. It's clearly all of the above.

So we're reading this novel, right? It's fairly good so far. The protagonist has some pretty weighty matters he needs to think about; maybe he's finding himself doing something he knows he shouldn't, or maybe he's seeking wisdom. At the height of his dilemma he steps into a church or Bible study and listens to a sermon. Would you believe that what the pastor says is exactly what he needed to hear? The text of this message contains chapter and verse for what the hero ought to do. He leaves the church relieved that God has solved his dilemma for him.

Well, doesn't this happen in real life? Don't we sometimes hear God's voice as we're listening to a sermon, even if what God tells us doesn't have direct bearing on what the speaker is actually talking about? Of course. That's one of the reasons we go to church, after all. So what's the issue?

My issue is that this makes for bad fiction. Overly convenient fiction. Just because something happens in real life doesn't mean it will work in fiction. Or are you ready to describe your characters' every trip to the bathroom? *That* happens in real life.

By the way, this chapter also refers to Bible study lessons, Sunday school lessons, and other long passages of this-is-just-what-he-needed-to-hear content. And it applies whether the sermon comes in the middle of the novel or at the beginning or end.

HOW CONVENIENT

Including a sermon in the middle of a novel is a bad idea for a number of reasons. It's a bad idea because it stops the story and makes the reader listen directly to the author. There's a reason kids squirm in church: It's boring to them. Making a reader sit through a full sermon is the equivalent of asking a five-year-old to stay interested in the adult pastor's sermon. The typical reader won't be able to do it and won't try.

It's a bad idea because the reader feels preached at. This is where it begins to feel like agenda-driven fiction. If you are thinking, "My goal for this book is to get today's young people to see that Facebook is evil, and if they're not going to go to church to hear it, I'm going to bring the sermon to them and package it in a story they'll like," your book is in big trouble. If the reader wants a sermon, she'll go to church. She doesn't want a sermon in a novel.

It's a bad idea to include a sermon in a novel because it's cheating. Instead of having the protagonist come to this crucial realization through the action of the story, you just put it all on a silver platter for him. This is outright *telling*, and it will kill your story's momentum. It's lazy storytelling.

It's a bad idea to include a sermon in a novel because it's a cliché. Oh, great, he's heading to a church. What do you bet he hears a sermon that contains the answer he's been searching for? Been there, done that. No, thank you.

It's a bad idea to include a sermon in a novel because it's a form of *deus ex machina*. The protagonist doesn't have to figure anything out for himself; God reaches down and hands him the perfect solution to the problem.

Does this mean you can't bring your protagonist near a church? Does it mean you can't have sermons taking place in your story? No and no. Your protagonist can spend the entire story inside a church if you want, and sermons can be going on 24/7.

Just don't include the text of those sermons in the story.

Now, you can have the pastor say something that strikes a chord in the protagonist's mind. In that case, include *that statement only* and summarize (or skip) the rest.

HIDDEN AGENDA

If your reason for writing a book is to tell people how bad something is, consider writing an article instead of a novel.

I can't tell you how many times I've read something like this in the fiction proposals I've considered over the years: I wrote this novel to prove Christians ought not gossip. ... My aim is for readers to conclude that unconfessed sin can cause their lives to fall apart. ... I have written this novel to show the complete depravity of man and that the world's only hope is salvation in Jesus Christ.

Don't get me wrong, I agree with all those things, especially the last one. But when it comes to fiction, *you can't write a novel to prove a point*. You can't be writing a sermon (or, more commonly, a diatribe) to tell off those accursed sinners.

Many well-meaning writers come to fiction as a means of sugar-coating their bitter pill. They want to preach to some deluded audience or rail against some social ill, and they feel fiction will somehow make their message more palatable and persuasive.

Agenda-driven fiction is bad for two reasons. First, it's almost always written by someone who has no interest in learning the craft of fiction. In other words, it stinks as a novel. These authors aren't typically patient enough to learn how to do it right. They just want to loose their fusillade and sail on with their lives.

Second, agenda-driven fiction is often bad because it isn't about a person or a story—it's about an important lesson. In fiction, story is king. It outranks everything else, including that lesson you want to drive into the reader's thick head.

Readers do not come to fiction to be preached at. They come for escape and entertainment and fun. You start putting in anything that feels like bony finger-pointing, and the reader will quickly find something else to do besides read your book. If they want a sermon, they'll go to church. Outside of church they don't want sermons.

BUT WHAT ABOUT THEME AND MESSAGE?

Am I saying that fiction must be about funny or entertaining things, "lite" topics without any substance? Of course not. Good novels have a theme or a message or even a note of warning or challenge. Hopefully your novel will have this, too.

My novels *Operation: Firebrand—Crusade* and *Operation: Firebrand—Deliverance* tackle serious humanitarian issues: modern slavery in Sudan and North Korean tyranny to its people, respectively. I wanted to make people aware of what's going on in these regions. But even in those novels, story was king, and characters reigned over message.

There's a difference between writing a novel to prove a point and writing a novel about a person and finding out later you've made an interesting commentary on some theme that resonates with you and readers.

Don't come to fiction to prove a point or teach a lesson. Just tell your story and let the chips fall where they may.

IF THE USHERS WOULD NOW PLEASE COME FORWARD

This chapter, like pretty much all of them in this book, is not law. It's my recommendation. If you feel you must have a sermon in your story somewhere, then by all means, put it in.

But in my opinion a sermon is near the top of the list of things not to include in a Christian novel. It's boring, it's lecturing, it's too convenient, it's lazy, it's a cliché, and it incinerates your story's momentum in a hail of fire and brimstone.

chapter 21
THE BAD BOY GETS SAVED—THE END

The final no-no we'll look at is probably the oldest and worst cliché in Christian fiction. Usually it's a story about a good church girl who falls in love with the local bad boy (who is inevitably named either Damien or Devlin). He's rakishly handsome, of course, but forbidden because he's a heathen.

Throughout the book the heroine reaches out to this lost soul with the Good News, to no avail. Meanwhile, our lusty heroine is fighting her own temptations to throw off all restraint while she simultaneously doubts God's goodness.

Just when it looks like our good girl is going to do the right thing and turn away from her heart's desire in order to stay pure, God removes the scales from Damien/Devlin's eyes, and he is radically saved.

Now he's off the "Thou Shalt Not" list, and she can marry him.

It's not always a romance that commits this no-no. Sometimes it's a godly mother praying for her prodigal son, a godly wife praying for her straying husband, or a wealthy but sad widower praying for that cute young woman at Starbucks he wants to date.

Whatever the case, the happy ending of the story is when the targeted person gets the clue and comes to Christ.

Don't do that. Don't let your happy ending be the lost person finding salvation.

The fact that it's a cliché ought to be reason enough to steer you away from such a thing in your novel. But the main problem with it is that such a portrayal gives a false picture of Christianity. A lost character becoming a Christian is a realistic happy ending to a book about as much as Cinderella getting married to the prince is a realistic happy ending to a movie. It makes for a nice, tidy story, but it doesn't reflect reality. Marriage is hard, even in fiction. So is the Christian life.

Sometimes Christian novelists, in their zeal to reach readers with the gospel, do those very readers a disservice. If we depict Christianity as the all-happy, end-all solution to life's problems, what will happen if someone takes our advice and becomes a Christian based on our recommendation? When that person discovers the bills don't get miraculously paid, the disease doesn't magically disappear, and Mr. or Mrs. Right doesn't instantly come along, what will happen to that person's faith?

It's been my experience that a person becomes a Christian when his problems *start*. Suddenly he appears on the devil's radar, and Big D sends a boatload of troubles his way to discourage him about this new Christianity thing.

In my six novels I've had exactly two people get saved. In both trilogies it happened in book 3 after both the character and the reader have had a good long time to see what real Christianity looks like in the lives of other characters. And in both instances life doesn't get instantly better for the person who's just come to Christ. In the first one in particular, his life gets miserable pretty quickly after singing "I Surrender All."

It's not wrong to show characters seeing the light and coming to Christ in your fiction. Just don't depict it as an "and they lived happily ever after" ending. Walking with Christ is hard and lonely and doesn't usually go with any miraculous change in the person's life circumstances.

There is, for the Christian, an ultimate happy ending, of course. Just don't let coming to Christ be the happy ending in your Christian novel. Right now, when you're strategizing your book, is the best time to think about what you're going to do with your ending.

CONCLUDING PART II

Are you feeling strategic? Like an eagle soaring over your story, seeing everything clearly, making sense of the whole while the poor, earthbound creatures below have no idea what's going on? I hope so!

In Part I we worked to get you centered in Christ as you sit down to write. In Part II we thought about the big picture: who you are as a novelist and what your story is going to be. Now we're ready to look at how to actually write this thing. Part III is all about the craft of writing Christian fiction. It's the heart of this book. We'll look at showing versus telling, description, dialogue, point of view, and dozens of other principles to guide you as you're creating your novel.

So roll up your sleeves and let's get to work.

PART III

WRITING YOUR NOVEL

chapter 22

STARTING YOUR BOOK

One day I went to the library and pulled five novels from the shelf. They were all in the genre I wanted to read, they were all about the right length for what I was looking for, and they each had a good cover and an interesting premise. I took them to a table and read the first paragraph of each.

I put all of them back except one. Only one engaged me right away. Only one of these authors realized you have to grab your reader in the first line, or you will lose her.

When I evaluate manuscripts, I pay close attention to how the book begins. I look very closely at the first line. Then I attend to the first half page. It is a rare author who has done a good job in these crucial few lines, and yet their power to snare or miss a reader is paramount.

Let's take a minute to look at how to start your book.

TO PROLOGUE OR NOT TO PROLOGUE

I have a dear friend and wonderful fiction teacher who urges her writing students not to include a prologue in their novels. Prologues, she says, are almost always telling and virtually never start a book out right—especially prologues written by beginning authors. Better to cut them and get on with the story.

My friend and I have had a wonderful time discussing this issue. I, a staunch advocate of prologues, once had students at a writers' conference come from her class to mine and tell me all my talk about writing prologues was confusing because this other teacher said not to do them.

There are two solutions to this dilemma. One is to realize that not all writing teachers agree. That should be freeing to you, actually. Go with the ones whose teaching makes the most sense to you. Second, we can arrive at a stance that takes both legitimate viewpoints into consideration.

My friend is correct: Most prologues are telling (exposition) and therefore slow the story down. A prologue full of telling is what ends up on the page when a novelist does not resist the urge to explain everything up front to the reader. Prologues often a way of dumping information about the history of a fictional world onto the reader. In this case, it is absolutely appropriate to delete the entire prologue and start when the story begins.

In my view, though, the problem isn't that the book had a prologue. The problem was that the author began with telling. You could simply swap out "Prologue" with "Chapter 1" and leave in all the telling, after all.

If you want a prologue, put one in. But whether you've got one or not, be sure to start your story with something *engaging*—and leave the telling untold.

Prologues are a great place to introduce your villain, establish the danger, and get the time bomb ticking. It's a freebie scene that can feature some character other than your main protagonist, because once your story proper begins, you'll want to stay with your main character's storyline for a good long time. The prologue is a good place to do nonprotagonist things early in the story.

THE FIRST LINE

I give a lot of attention to first lines. They are a very quick indicator of an author's skill level. Too many novels begin with someone pulling up in a car or with a weather report. Often they begin with telling: "Jim had always been a shy boy." Or else the first line will be trying to do too much at once: "Jim's long beard dripped with gravy from the state dinner with the Russian ambassador as he punched in the code to defuse the bomb planted there by the female Ukrainian terrorist who was so beautiful it broke Jim's already trampled heart."

Let your first line be three things: *simple, engaging, and appropriate to set the tone for the rest of the book*. You get only one first line. It has the most impact of any sentence in your entire book. Don't fritter it away.

Why simple? You want to grab your reader by the mind and pull her into your book; you want to make it an easy access.

The first line is the door to your store. If you've got an automatic door that slides aside to welcome the shopper, you're doing well. If you've got a manual door that sticks and rattles, you're not doing so well. Same with your book. The first line shouldn't be a tripping hazard.

Why engaging? As I illustrated with my visit to the library, many readers won't give you beyond that first line to get them hooked. Your first words had better be interesting. Look at the first sentence of something you've written—is it engaging? Does it suck the reader in?

Keep in mind that your first line is probably the most impactful sentence in the entire manuscript. What you do here resonates through the rest of your book. You're setting the tone, creating reader expectation, and starting your book out right.

A simple and engaging first line isn't going to help you if it doesn't set the right mood for what follows. If your novel is a light read about raising a delightful toddler, then beginning with, "Jim killed seven men that year," probably wouldn't start things out the way you want. Nor would, "The cancer had reduced her to a pathetic shell." Or, "Yes, sir, Sergeant Major, sir!"

Your book might be better served by something that lets the reader know she is, indeed, inside a light read. If you want a sunny tone for your book, be sure your first line is nice and sunny. Conversely, if you write a book about Jim's serial murders, then starting it with, "Say 'Goo-goo' for the camera, honey," probably won't work either.

Your first line needs to be right for the story you're telling. It also needs to engage. And it needs to be an uncomplicated sentence.

Here's one of my best first lines:

> Once he decided to kill himself, the rest was easy.

What do you think? Is it engaging? I hope so. Is it simple? Sure. Only one word over two syllables, and pretty short. And is it appropriate for the tone of the story? It's from my first novel, *Virtually Eliminated*, which is about a high-tech serial killer, so, yes, it's appropriate.

Here's another of my strongest first lines:

> Today I'm going to kill a man in cold blood (from *Operation: Firebrand*).

Who is this person? Who is he going to kill? And in cold blood? That's awful. What's happening? Something like this grabs the audience's attention.

It passes the engaging test, in other words. It's also another simple sentence. It glides right along and reads smoothly. Lastly, since it's about a Navy SEAL sniper on an assassination mission—who is becoming conflicted about his job—it's definitely appropriate for the story.

Those are good first lines. It also doesn't hurt to make your first line be about life and death, by the way.

So turn now to your current project. How does your first line stack up? How can you make it simple, engaging, and appropriate?

THE FIRST PAGE

All right, you've got a killer first line now. If you've done your job right, your reader will sprint to the second sentence and rush down the first page, fully hoping for you to really suck her into your book. In order to do that, you must begin with action.

But don't panic if you're a romance writer or women's fiction author. When I say, "Start with action," I don't mean you have to blow something up. It doesn't have to be an action sequence, per se. It just needs to be something *interesting* to the reader. Something engaging.

Your opening scene should involve someone *doing* something. Acting on a decision or executing a plan or committing a crime or attempting to win a game. If you're including a prologue, the opening scene *is* the prologue. As I mentioned, it's a great place to establish your villain and the stakes of your story, and to get the ticking time bomb going.

If you're not using a prologue, the opening scene ought to establish your protagonist's essential character quality. It ought to be a scene that brings your hero onstage in a way that perfectly typifies her for the reader (see Chapter 15). This, too, should be active and engaging.

What you don't want to start with is a full page (or more) of telling. Your reader doesn't care about the history of the pine valley. She doesn't care that when Susie was born she had a cat named Flo. Nor does she care to learn about all of Bobby's secret longings.

The reader wants to be engaged in a good story. So forget the trivial and begin with something interesting to hook your reader.

THE NEXT PAGES

You've got a great first line, and your opening scene runs at a great clip. Now what? More of the same, of course!

Good novels begin as I've described; agents and acquisitions editors often reject novels that don't begin quickly.

The following is a list of things to consider avoiding in your first forty pages. (And so long as you're avoiding them in the first pages, why not avoid them in the whole book?)

AVOID LOW STAKES

You need to establish early in your book what the "or else" consequences will be if the hero doesn't succeed in his goal. If the stakes are absent, or simply lame, the reader won't care about your story or your hero's plight.

Absent stakes are when the author expects us to just read about this interesting (to the author, at least) person who apparently doesn't want anything and is in no danger of something unpleasant happening if he doesn't accomplish it. Low stakes are when the hero wants something, but it's so mundane and boring the reader doesn't care.

Now, that's not to say your protagonist should always be trying to save the universe. Stakes can feel high to the reader even if what the hero wants is something that might otherwise feel small. As long as it's important to the protagonist, and as long as the reader feels connected to the protagonist, the stakes will be important to the reader.

How are the stakes in your book? Are they established early on? Are they something that will be sure to make the reader care enough about them?

AVOID LOW CONFLICT

Who or what stands opposed to what the protagonist wants?

Your hero, as the old adage goes, is only as strong as your antagonist. A wimpy antagonist (or an easily achievable goal) means the protagonist didn't have to be very heroic to overcome.

If the beginning of your book is about whether or not your character will or won't get up and answer the phone, it might not be especially engaging to the reader (unless the character is wounded or has some other true obstacle she has to overcome to get to the phone). Fiction is about conflict. It's about someone who wants something but is blocked from getting it by some obstacle or opponent.

What's your hero up against? Make sure it's a serious opponent or obstacle, or you won't have stakes, suspense, or conflict. Or an interested reader. You find your conflict by figuring out what stands in the way of what your hero wants. And you find out what your hero wants by reading Chapter 14.

AVOID GOING INTO A FLASHBACK TOO EARLY

I pretty much despise flashbacks. I know they can be marvelous tools in the hands of a master storyteller, and I realize this is just my personal opinion, but there has been only one unpublished manuscript I've ever seen that used flashbacks well. All the others that used flashbacks (and we're talking hundreds) did so in a way where the flashbacks were nothing but *telling.*

If you must use a flashback, don't do it in the first fifty pages of your book. Please. The reader hasn't gotten grounded yet in *this* story and *this* time frame before then, so she can't bear being yanked into another time frame with, possibly, a whole new set of characters. It's too early.

And please don't have some horrible thing happen and then reveal that it was only a dream (or a flashback). Talk about your fiction clichés.

Why do you feel you must use a flashback? To explain something to the reader? If that's your reason, just say no. Explaining is telling, and ... well, read "Focus on the Craft: Showing vs. Telling."

Whatever needs to come out about your story or main character can and should come out organically through the action of the tale you're telling right now. Consult the dumb-puppet trick (Chapter 31) for good ideas on how to do this without resorting to a flashback.

AVOID JUMPING TO A NEW VIEWPOINT CHARACTER TOO EARLY

In the same way that a reader can't bear jumping to a new timeline before she's grounded in your story, she also can't bear seeing through someone else's eyes too early in the story. It is my opinion that it works very well to stick with one viewpoint character *and one storyline* for at least the first forty to fifty pages of your book to give your readers time to ground themselves in your primary story and main protagonist.

These first forty pages are when you get your reader invested in the story. This is where you hook her to stick around for the whole book. Cut away too early and she'll spit out the hook and go on her way. (More about sticking with one storyline for the first forty pages in the next chapter.)

Authors often think that throwing in lots of variety early on, including a variety of viewpoints and storylines, will engage the reader. Unfortunately, doing so has the reverse effect. The reader doesn't know what's going on, whose story this is, or whom to pull for. It's disorienting.

Now, you can do a prologue from a viewpoint other than your protagonist's point of view. The reader can handle this because she understands that this prologue is something she'll need to know about later, and she trusts you to fill her in about it later. It can work to build suspense and establish your ticking time bomb, and it doesn't disorient the reader.

But once you get going in the main story with the main viewpoint character, don't break away for a good long time.

AVOID THE LACK OF ADEQUATE DESCRIPTIONS

I'm of the school of thought that says you should describe your characters and, even more important, your settings, and that you should describe them *well* and *early*.

If I, as an acquisitions editor, got two or three pages into someone's sample chapters and I still had no idea where the action was taking place—how many people were there, what anyone looked like, whether it was day or night, or any of the rest of what you're supposed to cover in basic description—I would probably put the proposal away and start working on my rejection letter.

Excluding description prevents you from thrusting your reader into your scene. And a reader not thrust into your scene is a disengaged reader, one who puts down your book and looks for something that will engage her. (Much more about description in "Focus on the Craft: Description.")

DEEPER INTO THE STORY

In this chapter we've looked at how to get your novel started with a bang. You've learned what to do and what to avoid in those crucial first pages. I've also just begun to introduce a number of topics we'll discuss as we move into the body of this section and the body of your book: showing versus telling, description, flashbacks, etc.

But those first pages are important to your book. They're all you have to engage a reader. And, before that, they're all you have to engage an agent or acquisitions editor. Whatever good things you learn to do in fiction, be sure you do them all in these first forty pages.

chapter 23

STAY WITH ONE STORYLINE BEFORE CUTTING AWAY

Most modern novels have more than one storyline. Maybe there are co-protagonists or a hero and a villain, and the story intercuts between them.

This is a terrific tool for the novelist. If one storyline is going to be slow for a while—say the hero is on a transpacific flight during which nothing happens to advance the story—it's wonderful for the author to be able to cut away to another storyline. She can go from one interesting, plot-advancing scene to another, with never a dull moment.

However, as great as this technique is, you can't hop around to different storylines too early in your book. You must let your reader get acquainted with the main storyline first. It is my opinion you should stay with your main storyline for a number of pages (forty to sixty) before cutting away to other storylines. And I'm talking about the *first* forty to sixty pages of your book—with the possible exception of a prologue.

HERE'S WHY

When your reader comes to your book, she needs a while to get grounded in your story's world and in your viewpoint character's mind. Cut away to another storyline too early, and it will have a disorienting effect on your reader.

Your poor reader was just beginning to catch your rhythm and figure out who the main character was and what that character was like. She was just beginning to care about your protagonist and become willing to invest in him. Suddenly that's yanked away from her, and she's asked to take on a whole new set of characters and concerns, a new viewpoint character, and a new major character and all that goes with that. She hasn't had time to really connect with your first one, and now she's expected to connect with a new one?

Except now she's gun-shy and afraid to engage with this new character because *this* one's probably going to get yanked away, too. So she stays aloof from your story. Fool her once, shame on you; fool her twice ...?

A reader who is wary of engaging with your book is a reader who is already 99 percent of the way to putting your book down permanently.

A NIGHT AT THE MOVIES

Imagine if you were selected to receive a free movie ticket at your local multiscreen Cineplex. You're assigned a burly escort, who leads you to a front-row seat in their shiny new stadium-seating auditorium. You sit through the forty-five minutes of premovie ads and previews, and finally the feature film begins. It looks good. This is the kind of movie you like. You settle in to have a g—

Your escort yanks you out of your chair and pulls you to the theater exit. What's going on? He drags you across the hall and into the movie that's playing there. He drops you into the front-row seat just as this other movie is beginning.

Flustered and a little angry, you try to go back to the first theater, but he won't let you. With a heavy sigh you turn your attention to the screen and try to get into this new movie.

Well, at least it's a comedy. And it has one of your favorite actors in it. You begin to think you might actually enj—

Yank. Dragged out. New theater. New movie.

Would you *cut that out?*

And so it goes. Just as you're getting into a story, you're asked to start caring about a new one. Sometimes you circle back to ones you've been in before, but by now you've been abused too much to care. You were never allowed to invest in any of the stories, so now they're all just noise. You don't care about any of them. And yet you could have. That's the tragedy.

It's jarring to go from storyline to storyline. As I mentioned at the outset, this is a tool used all the time by modern novelists, but it has to be set up right. You have to first give your reader an anchor, a home base, the understanding of whose story this really is. If you don't, she will feel jerked around like our poor moviegoer.

The trick is to *give* her a home base, and you do that by staying in your primary storyline, with your primary protagonist, for a good number of pages at the beginning of your book. I recommend at least forty contiguous pages before cutting away to another storyline.

This allows your reader to figure some things out, to get her bearings. It tells her who your protagonist is, what his or her main concerns, characteristics, goals, fears, and weaknesses are, and what kind of story this is. It introduces the main world of your story and, most likely, begins to sketch out what the story is going to be. It plants your reader firmly into your main character's mind.

Once she has that kind of grounding, you can cut away to other storylines to your heart's content. And cut away you should, for the reasons I outlined at the opening of this chapter.

WHY DO NOVELISTS CUT AWAY TOO EARLY?

I suspect novelists who cut to new storylines and viewpoint characters too early are doing so because they want to keep things interesting. They want the book to feel like it's moving along briskly—and besides, they're imitating what's being done in their favorite books and movies.

Good idea and good instincts, but wrong timing. Let your reader find her footing in your primary storyline before cutting away to any others.

The one exception to this rule, as I mentioned, is the prologue. Readers understand a prologue may be from a storyline other than the primary one, so they can handle it when chapter one is in a new storyline. It's like a freebie.

In a prologue, readers often get a tantalizing look at the devious madman who will be the book's antagonist, or they may learn what the "or else" component is as they see the villain start the time bomb to ticking, or they may see something that happened to the protagonist years before the primary story begins.

The point is that the reader is fine with not knowing everything that's going on in a prologue. If she's a little disoriented in a teaser scene like this, she can take it. In fact, she likes it, especially if the scene is well done and whets her appetite for what is to come.

People have brought to my attention many novels that violate this "rule" and go on to sell very well. That's why I say this is my opinion and preference, not a law. If you don't mind such things *as a reader*, and if such novels do keep you engaged even when they're jumping around very early, then by all means use such a device in your own fiction.

But here's a suggested plan: *Do* intercut between multiple storylines, but begin with the primary one and don't cut away from it for at least forty pages (except in the case of a prologue). A special case is the giant epic with twenty different storylines and viewpoint characters. That takes some careful balancing and is the topic of our next chapter.

chapter 24
WHOSE EPIC IS THIS?

When it comes to writing fiction there are very few formulas that can be brought to the task. Fiction is, after all, a nonscientific process that defies quantification and mathematical scrutiny.

However, there are some rules of thumb that can be helpful to any novelist. We saw one in Chapter 13, for instance, which explains when and why people (even fictional characters) change. These few formulae are tools and guidelines, though. Never laws.

In this chapter I will introduce you to a formula that can help you be sure your reader knows whose story this is and who the main protagonist is.

Most times this isn't a problem. It's clear from the beginning who the main character is and what the main story is going to be. But other times—such as when you're telling an extremely complex epic with many viewpoint characters or when you're writing a middle book in a series—it can be hard for your reader to know what's going on.

And few things frustrate a reader more than not being able to understand what she's looking at. The reader needs to know, almost from page one, whose story this is.

Your reader, you see, desperately wants to engage with your story. She wants to invest herself into the life of a sympathetic protagonist. She wants to care about your hero, in other words. And you need to let her know whose story this is so she can start the process of knitting her heart to that character.

I said you should start this *almost* on page one, because there's room for a prologue that features another character or characters, possibly the antagonist, especially if it establishes the stakes and sets the ticking time bomb. But after that, I feel you need to get your reader oriented into the life and vulnerability of your protagonist.

In a traditional novel you'd include the prologue to establish the "or else" stakes, and then you'd begin chapter one with a Chapter 15-style introduction of your central protagonist. After that, you'd give us at least forty pages of that character's storyline before cutting away. Only after page fortyish should you introduce a new storyline and begin cutting back and forth between them for the rest of the novel.

But let's say you're writing a very complex story with four, seven, or even as many as a dozen viewpoint characters. It's an epic, of course, and an epic often has many storylines so the reader can get a feel for the massive scope of the story.

If this is you, remember one thing: Your book still needs to be about *one main character.* Yes, it's about all those other people, too, but not in the ultimate sense. Ultimately, this has to be the story of one character on an inner and outer journey to try to achieve some objective.

Who is your story about? Who is your main hero?

The Lord of the Rings is about Frodo. Period. The original *Star Wars* series (Episodes IV, V, and VI) is about Luke Skywalker. The whole six-plus-movie series is about Anakin Skywalker/Darth Vader. Sure, lots of other characters figure prominently in these beloved stories, but there is still a central character and a main storyline.

So it must be with your epic. The reader must be able to know whose story it is, despite a supporting cast of thousands.

It's tempting to keep "entertaining" the reader by introducing a new viewpoint character and a new storyline every ten pages or so. I mean, why not? Right away the reader gets the idea that this is a huge story. Right away the reader is wowed by your many locations and situations. And look at how quickly you've brought everyone onstage and gotten the various storylines going.

But that's a mistake. It could be a fatal mistake, in terms of whether or not your reader will be able to stick with you as you jump from one protagonist to another. What you gained in flooding the page with characters, you more than lost in reader engagement. The poor reader is drowned, plunged under the tsunami of all your story people and all your storylines and all your story worlds.

You *must* allow your reader to get her bearings on the main story and the main protagonist before you introduce anyone or anything else. How long does it take a reader to gain that anchor hold? At least forty pages. That's forty unbroken, contiguous pages about your main character and the main storyline.

This doesn't mean, incidentally, that the hero has to be onstage alone. You can bring in the whole constellation of characters who revolve around her and through whose world she travels. But in terms of viewpoint character, for the first forty pages you must have only one.

You can bring other viewpoint characters and their stories online soon, but not before you hand the reader a lifeline—the main character. In effect, you are telling her that no matter what happens or how confused she gets she can always know *this* is the main person she needs to pay attention to.

AND NOW THE FORMULA

Let's say you have six major viewpoint characters in your epic. You now know that you need to introduce the main one first (possibly after a prologue), but how and when do you bring in the others without confusing the reader? And how often do you keep coming back to the main storyline? Here's where my formula will help.

I have presented the formula as an outline. It's not to be taken legalistically, of course, but it could serve as your template. Once you see what it's doing, you can try altering it, but first try to match it pretty much exactly. Consider structuring your epic according to this blueprint:

- Prologue (in which you do establish stakes, introduce the antagonist, and start the time bomb to ticking)
- Give us, your readers, forty contiguous pages in the main protagonist's storyline. (Begin with a Chapter 15 introduction and then launch the main story; be sure to show the character's flaw as described in Chapter 12.)
- Pick your second most important viewpoint character (preferably one who would be a nice counterpoint to the main one, and possibly the romantic lead) and give us twenty to twenty-five pages introducing that character and storyline.
- Then go back and give us ten to eighteen pages *in the original storyline* (this is to reestablish it as the main story and to reas-

sure the reader she does know what's going on; coming back to a storyline you have introduced, after being away, is psychologically comforting to the reader).

- Give us ten to fifteen pages introducing your *third* storyline and set of characters.
- Circle back to the secondary protagonist for ten pages or so.
- Follow with a solid twenty to twenty-five pages in the main-viewpoint character's story.
- Now pick your fourth most important viewpoint character and introduce him or her in fifteen pages or so.
- Circle around for ten-page scenes in storylines two and three.
- Follow with a major scene in the main protagonist's storyline (you're keeping all the plates spinning, you see).
- Then you can introduce your fifth storyline.
- Follow with an update from at least one of the other storylines.
- Then you can introduce your sixth storyline.
- Follow with a major scene from your main storyline.
- And then add updates from the others.

From here on, you can jump happily between all your storylines. Just be sure to circle back often (and for longer visits) to what's happening with your main character.

Give the reader a good long time to get connected with the person whose story this is and keep going back to that person. This is who your reader thinks your book is about, so it needs to be about him. Even with this, you'll also see I was able to bring on five other viewpoint characters and never cause the reader to feel the book has become about someone other than the main person she has bonded with.

The idea is to keep your primary hero before the reader's eyes longer and more often than any other viewpoint character. By continuing to circle back to that one, you reassure her that the author hasn't forgotten whom the reader is most attached to.

And you do the same thing at a smaller scale with each of the other storylines. It's a lot of balls to keep in the air, but as in real juggling each one has to be given the right amount of attention at the right time to keep it all working.

CHAPTER ONE DOMINATES ALL

And now a word about what you include in chapter one of your epic. Be sure it's a scene featuring your main protagonist and it's from the primary storyline. Chapter one, you see, is more powerful than any other chapter in your book.

You know how baby animals supposedly imprint on whatever creature they see when they're first born or hatched? Readers are like that. Whatever they see in chapter one, they take to heart. They imprint on it like a baby bird just out of the shell. They assume that this is the main character, the one they're supposed to engage with. And so they do.

If you've got a massive story with tons of viewpoint characters, resist the urge to get them all in front of the reader at once. You've got to let her know whose story this really is. Once she knows that, you can begin to slowly add on new ones.

In the TV show *Lost*, the writers stuck with the first (large) set of characters for the whole first year. It wasn't until we well and truly knew them that we could bear the addition of new characters. We had to keep seeing our favorites, of course, but we could handle some new ones because we had a good sense of who our main ones were. Every season after, the writers brought in new characters. We could handle new characters because we had a good hold on who the primary group was.

So it should be in your epic.

EMPHASIS

In the world of fine art there is a principle known as *emphasis*. A picture must clearly indicate to the viewer what the main thing is. Should the viewer focus more on the girl or the flowers? In the text layout, the composition should reveal what words or letters have dominance. This is to clue the viewer in and to direct his eye.

A picture with no emphasis, one in which multiple items share equal prominence, is confusing and even irritating to the viewer. What's the main thing? It's impossible to tell. All the similarly emphasized objects cancel each other out, leaving the viewer unengaged and staring blankly at what could've been a new favorite work of art.

In art composition, you create emphasis through the use of contrast, placement, separation, color, focus, distance, and relative size. In fiction, you create emphasis by giving chapter one (and the first forty pages) to your main storyline and then circling back to it often.

Even an epic must have a focus.

Frodo lives.

Focus on the Craft:

SHOWING vs. TELLING

If there's one thing that sinks more fiction proposals than anything else, it's *telling*.

My pet name for telling is *blah, blah, blah*. You know that person you talk to—or, rather, listen to—who can go on for hours about nothing, talking nonstop and not letting you get a word in? That's telling: rabbit trails, endless detail about things you don't care about, expecting you to be interested in the third story of your neighbor's friend's cat.

You'd think novelists would know better than to bore their readers, but you'd be surprised. You'd think that novelists certainly wouldn't include material in their books that was the equivalent to a *Don't Read Me* sign, but you'd be mistaken.

Telling kills fiction, both in terms of story momentum and in terms of its chances of ever being published.

I know that many best-selling authors fill their books with telling. I've been told by many students: "Yeah, but so-and-so does it." My response is, "So?" Just because some people get by with bad habits doesn't mean you should adopt their bad habits. And it doesn't mean those bad habits are part of the reason for their success.

If they were to cut their telling, their books would improve. Same with yours.

The antidote to telling is what we call showing. Showing is to telling what TV is to radio. Better, showing is to telling what Blu-ray is to braille.

In this section, I will discuss all the pertinent aspects of showing versus telling.

chapter 25

WHAT IS SHOWING VS. TELLING?

In fiction, *telling* is giving information in a straight summarized fashion: "Jim was a lazy slob." *Showing* is illustrating that same content through scene, action, and dialogue. For instance, at home with Jim:

> "Louise, where's my beer? I'm thirsty, woman!"
>
> "Get off that couch and get it yourself, why don't you?"
>
> Jim scratched his belly and enjoyed how it jiggled like a water balloon. "Just get it, all right? Get it and I'll … I'll get out there and mow the front lawn."
>
> Louise poked her head around the doorjamb. "You mean today?"
>
> "Yes, today. What'd you think I meant?"
>
> "And you'd do the back lawn, too?"
>
> Jim pointed the remote and changed the channel. "Don't get greedy now."
>
> Louise went back down the hall. "Get your own beer."

You see it took a little longer to *illustrate* that Jim is a lazy slob than it did to simply feed it to the reader on a spoon, but the showing version is far more interesting.

We might know intellectually from the telling version that Jim is slovenly and lazy, but from the showing version we *feel* it. We know it in a deep way. Jim is a slob, a jerk, a lazy moron, and he treats his family like dirt. With showing, what you lose in brevity you gain in impact.

Showing is when you reveal things about your characters, the story world, relationships, etc., as you go about advancing your story.

With *telling*, you stop the story in its tracks, kill whatever momentum you had going, and back up like a dump truck to dump information onto your reader. When you do so, your reader thinks, "I don't care about this stuff right now! Get on with the story."

Telling bores your reader. Do you need any more motivation than that to eliminate it from your story?

Imagine you've gone to a movie theater, and the show starts. But instead of seeing anything on the screen, you're treated to fifteen minutes of a narrator droning on about the history of the characters. A black screen and boring voice-over for fifteen minutes. Are you going to sit there and watch that movie?

Finally something happens on the screen. You're getting interested and chalking up that weird opening to experimental cinema, when all of a sudden the screen goes black again, and the narrator starts up once more. Another fifteen minutes.

I don't know about you, but I wouldn't stand for that. I didn't come to listen to some boring guy explain everything. I came to *watch a story happen before my eyes*. I'm switching theaters or getting my money back.

That's what telling is in fiction. It's making your reader stare at a black screen while you narrate everything she "needs" to know to appreciate your book. Except she just flat doesn't care. She doesn't. She didn't come to understand the whole history of everything and everyone. She came to watch a story happen before her eyes.

Telling is narrating. Showing is turning the movie projector on and actually portraying a story with people and scenes. As an author, you need to think of yourself as a filmmaker, not as a boring, explaining, rabbit-chasing storyteller around the campfire.

CATEGORIES OF TELLING

There are three main areas in which novelists generally resort to telling: backstory, exposition, and explanation of character motivation. But they all have one thing in common: They stop the story cold and elicit snores from the reader.

Backstory is background information about your story, the environment, the setting, the characters, and the relationships. Here are some examples:

> Kevin had grown up in affluence. His parents had always given him whatever he wanted. So he was spoiled, too. When he was ten, his mother bought him a …

> The planet had been colonized two hundred years ago as part of the empire's sweeping plan to …
>
> Jerry used to be Susie's boyfriend, but that was before Susie caught Jerry kissing Delilah, who had been Tom's girl before the operation.

Do you see how the story has shifted into neutral (or park, or even reverse) while the author spoon-feeds the reader information about how things were before the story began? Nothing is actually happening. The story is stalled while we are forced to endure a lecture on the lore of yesteryear.

Backstory is similar to someone delaying the beginning of a movie in order to stand in front of the audience and say, "Before you can watch this you need to understand the distribution channels we went through to bring this to you. And you probably need to understand how distribution works in other industries besides the film industry. It all began back in …" The audience would revolt, shouting, "Shut up and get on with the story!"

Good advice.

Don't explain everything that happened before now. Resist the urge to "get everything on the table" for the reader. Don't front-load your story with explanation of that background.

The second category of telling is *exposition*. Exposition is when the novelist explains everything that's happening and why.

> The movers had used heavy-duty packing tape because sometimes the lighter stuff gave way and someone's belongings would come crashing to the floor.
>
> The events that took place over the next month were the strangest the town had ever known.

As Browne & King say in their fabulous book *Self-Editing for Fiction Writers*: "Resist the urge to explain." This kind of telling is like meta-information. It's information *about* the story rather than something in the story itself. Readers don't care. Don't explain everything.

Finally, telling happens in *character motivations* when the novelist caves in to the impulse to explain everything about her characters.

> "Oh, my!" Twilene was impressed with what the general had said. "I'm so impressed with what you just said, General!"

> "But everyone knows I'm not making this up, right?" Jerome said, looking for some support because he was feeling insecure.

Do you see how the character's motives were explained? "Lucy had a fear of being outside, so she always stayed indoors if she could." How boring is that? It's like cheating. You've communicated something interesting about your character, but you've done it in the most uninteresting way possible.

Worse, if you write it like that, it won't even impact the reader's mind. You might *tell* us that she's scared of the outdoors, but until you *show* her being afraid of going outside, we won't believe it.

Two other categories of telling are flashback and recap, which I'll discuss in later chapters.

DEATH TO TELLING

The irony is most of the time novelists later show what they've already told. They do both, like Twilene and Jerome above. If you cut the telling, wouldn't their words have *shown* the very thing the novelist felt compelled to also tell? You don't need both.

I believe novelists resort to telling because they're concerned the reader won't get the point if they don't. That's why I used telling in my early (and unpublished) years of writing, and it's why other novelists tell me they've put that stuff in. "I was afraid the reader wouldn't understand that they'd once had a relationship if I didn't spell it out."

And so we go on being heavy-handed and treating our readers like dimwits.

Meanwhile, once we think we've *told* them enough that they'll get it, we then proceed to *show* it, more confident that we'll be understood. But the truth is readers know how to interpret fiction. When you take out the telling, the showing remains. And that's all you need. You can remove just about every bit of telling in your book, and you'll find you've actually *shown* it adequately.

See how that works? Once the author feels she has gotten everything adequately explained so the reader won't be lost, she goes on with acting out her story. The irony is she didn't need to do the explaining at all, and if she were to remove it, she'd find she's actually included all the pertinent information in what she's *shown*.

A reader who understands something because you pound it into her with telling is going to feel like her brain has been turned off or numbed. It's like listening to a parental lecture. In contrast, a reader who "catches on" to something in your story from the way two characters talk or who figures something out based on the awards on a character's wall will feel engaged and energized.

Which do you want your reader feeling?

DON'T SUMMARIZE—DRAMATIZE! DON'T NARRATE—ILLUSTRATE!

Go back through your manuscript looking for the telling. It will be hard to see at first, but you must work to develop the ability to spot it. (More on spotting telling in your writing by spotting it in others' writing in Chapter 29.)

Where you do see it, consider cutting it out.

Without the exposition, is your story hurt? Does the reader not know something that she must know to understand the story? Probably not.

If so, if you've stumbled upon one of those rare occasions when something that you'd put into telling is actually necessary to the story, then you must figure out a way to bring that out through scene, action, and dialogue. In other words, make it part of the story. (One way to do that is the dumb-puppet trick: Chapter 31.)

Here's my suggestion: Include the bare minimum your reader needs to know to understand what's going on.

Remember our rabbit-chasing storyteller? Don't be like that. If the object is to talk about X, reveal to the reader everything she needs to know about X to understand your story. Don't tell the history of X, the motives of X, or the full life cycle of X. Just the facts.

But hold on: That doesn't mean you can give three pages (or even three sentences) of telling, so long as it's stuff the reader needs to know. No, it just means those are the bits you need to find ways to dramatize.

Don't summarize—dramatize! Don't narrate—illustrate!

When you're showing, you may feel you're speaking with a more limited vocabulary or painting with a broader brush than when you're telling. When you restrict yourself to only what the reader can catch by watching your story play out, it may feel more like a blunt instrument. After all, you've become accustomed to telling every last detail you could think of—and now you have to illustrate everything?

If you're feeling restricted, good! That's what discipline feels like. It means you're going to have to decide what things are really important and illustrate only those things. Back when you could throw in everything and the kitchen sink, you could be lazy and self-indulgent. Now you have to make hard choices.

Because it *is* harder to figure out how to convey something through scene, action, and dialogue than it is to just tell the reader exactly what you mean. Just for the sake of time and your sanity you'll find yourself tossing out the nonessentials and retaining only what needs to be there.

TELL ME MORE— NO, WAIT ... *SHOW* ME

Novelists sometimes worry that their word count will go down too far if they cut out those pages and pages of momentum-killing telling. It's the first ten pages of their book! How can they cut that? Or they may worry that their word count will go *up* too high if they write out into full scenes all the information they'd originally given on a platter.

The truth is that the two will cancel each other out.

It's easier to tell, but if you give too much information, you stop the story, and you bore the reader. It's harder and takes more words to show instead, but you keep the story going and you cause your reader to engage in your book.

Are there exceptions? Is there ever a time when summary is okay or even preferred? Absolutely. Take a look at Chapter 30.

If you're a filmmaker, you are allowed to include only that which the camera can see and the microphone can hear. When you think about it that way, all those pages of nothing but narration in which you're explaining the world and its history will seem out of place. How can you do *that* with only a camera and microphone? You can't. So cut it.

You can't push the analogy too far, of course, because fiction allows us to see through the eyes and hear the thoughts of our viewpoint characters, which film usually can't do. But it is still a useful rule of thumb.

Go forth!

Okay, time for you to go hunting for the telling in your manuscript. As you go, watch out for the little sneaky ones, too, like:

> "I did," said the plumber who had once been a sailor in the navy. "I surely did."

When you find the telling, delete it. That will probably be all you need to do, as you've likely *shown* the same information elsewhere. If you find you need a bit of what you've cut, figure out a way to dramatize it in a scene.

To get started, rent Hitchcock's *Rear Window* and watch the opening camera move that pans across the inside of our protagonist's apartment. Before a single word is uttered, you know a ton about this guy. That, my friend, is showing.

chapter 26
FLASHBACKS

Nine times out of ten, flashbacks are just another form of telling.

They are further examples of the author trying to explain everything, perhaps the history of why a character acts in a certain way. To her credit, she's trying to put it into a scene instead of on a spoon, but it's still not information the reader cares about, and it's still stopping the main story. That makes it telling.

YEAH, BUT *THE NOTEBOOK* DOES IT

I know, I know: Some of the greatest literature of the English language is filled with flashbacks. I also know that some very popular novels in our era are told in flashbacks, like *The Notebook*. Furthermore, it is within my knowledge that many great movies use flashbacks, such as *Sunset Boulevard* and *Amadeus*.

If I have seen one hundred unpublished novels that make use of one or more flashbacks, and I've probably seen more than that, out of those only one or two actually worked. Beginning writers (and many published writers, it should be noted) may not be able to pull it off.

Usually a flashback is a dramatized information dump, but it's simply still an information dump. It's a Broadway cast performing the text of a soup label. You stop the story so you can explain background to the reader (who doesn't care, incidentally). It may be interesting as a scene, but it's still taking the reader away from the main story. And that's a bad thing, in my opinion.

Flashbacks fall into the same category as any other form of telling, and therefore the same questions apply. Does the reader really need to know this information to understand the story? Probably not. But if the reader does need to know it, can you come up with an organic and chronological way to *show* it through scene and dialogue? Most likely, yes.

Flashbacks, like the more mundane kinds of telling, are usually just exposition. They are the ultimate "backstory." But the reader simply doesn't need it.

Imagine if George Lucas had stopped *Star Wars* to go into flashbacks whenever a new character stepped onstage. Princess Leia appears—and suddenly we have to sit down and watch Episodes I, II, and III so we'll understand her backstory—and then we can go back and see what happened to her in the "present."

And what about the backstory of the people you saw in the flashback? Oh, no! What's *their* backstory? Gotta explain that. There's Darth Maul and the gray-haired adviser on Naboo, plus Anakin's mother. Where'd they all come from? What's their story?

Meanwhile we've all but forgotten that there was some princess in some other story way back at the beginning.

So then we get back into that story, but now there's this cowboy kind of guy in a cantina. What's *his* story? Let's go have a big long flashback.

Very quickly the movie would've bogged down and become ridiculous. But Lucas didn't do that, thankfully. Instead, he introduced his characters well and let the story unfold. As we went along, we learned more about the characters we cared about but never in a way that robbed the story of its momentum.

EITHER CUT IT OR FOLD IT INTO THE CURRENT STORY

So take a look at your work in progress. Do you have any flashbacks in it? Why? Is it truly because there is no other way in this particular quantum universe that information could be revealed? Or is it just a way of explaining everything to the reader so she has no questions about why Jimmy is limping or why Harriet won't talk to Laverne?

Judging from the flashbacks I've seen in the manuscripts I've worked with, I'd be willing to wager it might be the latter. You just want to explain it all. You know it, and you want the reader to know it, but you've been told that straight information dumps stop the story, so you've written this elaborate scene to bring it all onstage.

Except that while you are indulging your need to explain everything, you *have* stopped your story cold just as surely as if you'd just launched into pages of straight exposition: "She didn't like him because one day they …"

Remember Browne & King's maxim: Resist the urge to explain. A straight chronological layout for your story is almost always going to be best.

Think about your own story: Is there any reason you couldn't tell this story in order without resorting to time hopping? If you used the principles of *showing*, couldn't you organically bring out everything that needs to be brought out?

I urge you to remove all flashbacks from your story.

One possible exception might be a prologue that takes place several years earlier in the protagonist's life or in your story's world, if it sets up the villain, time bomb, stakes, or main problem of your story.

And there are certain stories that ought to be told in flashback or out of chronological order. *Memento* is a great example of a story that *had* to be told out of order, and *The Notebook* works well, too. But note that both stories involved brain damage or Alzheimer's, thus mandating the nonchronological order. Yours probably isn't like that.

I had the honor of editing the excellent novel *Marduk's Tablet* by T.L. Higley. In it a modern-day expert in ancient handwriting encounters an ancient tablet that, whenever she touches it, sends her back in time to see through the eyes of a treacherous Babylonian priestess. Throughout the manuscript we are jumping back and forth between the action in the historical storyline and the action in the present-day storyline. It totally worked.

Ted Dekker's Circle trilogy is like that, too, in that we're jumping back and forth between times and worlds.

Such books can get away with nonchronological storytelling because of their premise. But, like I said, yours most likely isn't like that. And even if it is, I'd advise you to keep the flashbacks to a minimum. On the other hand, if you love flashbacks in the fiction you read, by all means include them in the fiction you write.

Sometimes, though, you're better served by sticking to a straight, chronological telling of your story. Please consider removing and rewriting flashbacks.

Death to telling.

chapter 27

THE OL' HOP-OVER-IT-AND-RECAP-IT-LATER TRICK

The final category of telling to discuss is this, which I've given the oh-so-smooth title you see above.

Sometimes the novelist jumps beyond an important event in the lives of the characters—an event the reader very much wants to witness—and then has someone summarize what happened after the fact. She skips over the event and recaps it later.

I personally don't think this is a good idea. To me, it seems like it's telling, it's lazy, and it's awful. Beyond perhaps every other form of telling, this one is most irritating to your reader.

The little girl has been dreading her stage performance for weeks (and chapters). It's been the central thought on her mind for pages and scenes. She's been rehearsing, attempting to perfect her lines, working with the costumes and props, but everything she does seems to go wrong, and she simply can't get it right. Anxiety makes her sick every night and even during the day as the show date nears. She's praying and hiding and crying whenever she's not working on the project. Finally the big moment arrives, and she steps out onstage.

Then the scene ends.

In the next scene her mom is talking to someone on the phone. "Oh, yes, Doris, the show went great. She did fine. Everyone liked it. Once, she thought she was going to forget a line, but then she remembered it, and the rest went perfectly. She got roses."

Now, I don't know about you, but if I were to read that I would be very upset. The scene I'd been heading toward the whole time—anticipating, dreading, longing for, right along with the character—finally arrived. But somehow, despite my every effort, *I missed it*. It happened offstage. Are you kidding me? Then I have to read some after-the-fact summary of it?

I read every word of every previous page. I pulled for the little girl. I was beside her when she was sick with worry and fear. I willed her to remember her lines. And by doing those things, I earned a spot on the front row of the crucial scene. When she stepped on that stage—and at every moment through and beyond the crucial point—I wanted to be right there with her.

Instead, the novelist cheated me. I wanted with all my heart to see that scene happen, but I was kept on the outside as if I were a stranger or, worse, an enemy. And I'm mad at that author. (Note: An angered reader won't finish your book.)

The average reader may not realize why she's upset and feeling frustrated or let down, but this is why. She wanted to be front and center for the big event, but the author didn't let her see it.

It's like calling up your mother-in-law and saying, "Oh, by the way, your daughter's pregnant. Actually, she gave birth last month. Thought you'd like to know."

Skipping over the big event and telling about it in retrospect halts your momentum, disrespects and irritates your reader, and distances her from your story.

OKAY, BUT NOBODY DOES THAT, RIGHT?

I wish I could say that were true. I wish I could say that I've invented some obscure fiction sin that nobody ever commits. But that's not so. I see this all the time.

It is, after all, a lot easier to summarize *(tell)* a scene than to show it. And the more the important the scene, the more pressure there is to do it well. How much nicer it would be to not have to write it at all. *Aha!* the novelist thinks, *I'll just bring readers right up to the brink, skip over it, and summarize it later. That'll be a lot easier on me.*

I think novelists sometimes do this hop-over-and-recap-later thing out of some misguided sense of suspense. They realize this is a moment the reader wants, and they've learned that withholding from the reader the thing she wants is sometimes a good way to up the tension. So it follows that the ultimate way to up tension would be to completely withhold from the reader the thing the reader most wants to see. Great idea, huh?

Suspense isn't something withheld, it's something withheld *temporarily.* It's something you've had to wait and wait and wait for but that does finally come. Doing all this buildup without providing the reader with the big event she's been patiently waiting for is an extreme example of "plant without payoff" (which I cover in detail in Chapters 43 and 44). Don't do it.

DO THE WORK— WRITE OUT THE SCENE

You must not let things the reader wants to see take place offstage. If the event is important to a main character and falls within the scope of the current story, it's important to the reader and must therefore be *shown as a scene* in the book.

Imagine if all the X-wings took off toward the Death Star, and then we cut to the medals scene at the end. Someone comes into the hangar and says, "Boy, Luke, that was amazing. I didn't think you guys were going to make it, but you did it. And who would've guessed Han Solo would return like that? But what about Darth Vader? Isn't he still alive even though the Death Star is destroyed? Oh, and too bad about R2D2, but I think he's okay now. All right, go get your medal!"

That's an extreme example. But I wish I could say I'd not seen anything that egregious in the manuscripts I've worked with over the years.

Now, in fiction, don't we skip over some scenes? Of course! We don't write every scene for every major character. They have to go to the bathroom, for instance, but most readers don't want to see those scenes.

Nor do we have to show every major event in the main characters' lives. Okay, so she was orphaned at age three. That's a brutal tragedy, but if the story takes place much later in her life and does not involve her parents or early childhood, scenes like that don't have to be portrayed onstage in the current story.

But if it's something readers would reasonably want to see, if it's something involving a main character, and if it belongs within the purview of the current story, you must write out the full scene and let readers have front-row seats for the whole thing.

Or readers will start to dislike you. You'll be like the stepdad who promises a special thing but then forgets or simply doesn't deliver on the promise. Though they will want to like you, you will have caused them to understand that you will betray and disappoint.

That's not what you want your readers feeling about you and your story. Do the work. Write out the crucial scenes. Don't summarize—dramatize!

Write out *(show)* all the scenes your readers want to see. Let your readers in—like the most intimate of friends—to the secret fears and the moments of truth. And all will be well with the world.

All right, that covers the major categories of telling. Hopefully you've begun to spot some of these in your own manuscript and delete them.

Now let's look at a topic that sometimes confuses earnest novelists who wish to eliminate telling from their writing—and can end up going too far.

chapter 28

UNDERSTANDING THE DIFFERENCE BETWEEN DESCRIPTION AND TELLING

Sometimes authors hear my "death to telling" message, and they go back through their works in progress, cutting out every paragraph that looks suspiciously like telling. If that's you, bravo (or brava)! Your manuscript will be better for it.

But sometimes they find they've cut too much. It's not that some telling should've remained (see Chapter 30); it's that some of what they cut wasn't telling at all. Just because a paragraph isn't dialogue and isn't describing action doesn't automatically mean it's telling.

It might be description.

DESCRIPTION IS NOT TELLING

Description can feel an awful lot like telling. A paragraph describing a room looks like a paragraph of explanation, which now we know is a primary category of telling. So shouldn't it be cut? No.

Telling is something the story doesn't need. It's extraneous information the author felt like sharing—or it's something that ought to be fleshed out into a full scene. It's a movie with no movie, just a boring narrator.

Description, on the other hand, *is* the movie. It's what the camera sees and the microphone hears. It's the establishing shot. It's the depiction of what and who is there, what it smells like, what time of day it is, etc. It sets the stage so that the story may take place on it.

Description allows the reader to visualize the scene. *Telling* cheats the viewer of any visualization and replaces it with recap.

Now, if you hate description *as a reader*, then by all means leave description out of the fiction you write. I love description, but that's a personal preference.

Take a look at the following paragraph:

> Kevin stepped into his father's basement office. It was the size of a child's bedroom. French doors opened into the office, which had one window, a corner desk, and a single bookshelf. The most striking feature of the room were the walls, which looked to Kevin exactly like the surface of Mars: burnt orange and textured with bumps like satellite photos of the Red Planet. The oatmeal carpet was new but already had tufts of black cat hair visible on it, especially along the white baseboards. This was where the magic happened?

It kind of seems like this paragraph doesn't move the story forward. And if you're on the search for paragraphs of *telling* in your manuscript, this might be the kind of thing you'd be inclined to cut. Nothing happens. It's just excess fat that needs to be trimmed, right? Not so much.

Telling, as we've seen, consists of exposition, backstory, and explanation of motives (plus flashbacks and recaps). Telling stops the story to tell the reader something she doesn't need to know, just because the author can't bear not explaining everything.

On first glance, that's what the descriptive paragraph above looks like, but it's not. Description, unlike telling, represents something the reader *does* need to know: what the scene looks like, how many people are there, whether it's day or night, how big the room is, etc.

I'll go into much more detail about descriptions in "Focus on the Craft: Description," but for now know that you need to set the stage for the reader. If you don't, who will?

How can the reader imagine your scene if you don't describe it? If you cut out all your description, the reader draws a blank when trying to picture what's going on. It's incredibly irritating to your reader to not be able to generate a mental image of your story.

Telling stops the story. Description allows it to go forward.

It is essential to set the stage for your reader early in the scene. I recommend getting started on description at least by the bottom half of the first page of a new scene, if not sooner.

Doing so gives the reader the same information she'd get in the first seconds of footage in a movie. Failing to do so leaves her disoriented and floating in ether—and frustrated. That's more like creating an amateur radio drama than a movie. At least in professional radio they add sound effects and other clues to give you a sense of place. Many novelists don't even give you that.

Don't be afraid to describe your settings and your characters. You must do so. It's not telling. Without description your reader cannot imagine what's going on. And that stops the momentum of your story even worse than including a paragraph of telling.

You are the filmmaker for your story. If you do it without description, it's as if you're making a movie but not bothering to use a camera.

Description is not telling. Leave the description in. Cut the telling.

chapter 29
SPOT THE TELLING

This chapter title sounds like I'm telling you to be snarky about how inferior your fellow writers' fiction is, doesn't it?

That's not what I'm trying to say. We need to be as loving toward our fellow Christian novelists as we want them to be to us. No, what I'm talking about is different. I have come to realize that there is a step between understanding a fiction-writing concept—like showing versus telling—and being able to apply that concept to your own writing.

You may fully understand you shouldn't start your book with backstory, for instance, but when you look at your actual manuscript you can't see that's exactly what you've done. It's as if your own writing is invisible to you, impervious to your efforts to discern if you've followed or violated whatever rule of good craftsmanship you've tried to apply. Even if you're positive you completely understand that rule.

I realized it would be helpful to create an intermediate step between understanding the principle and being able to spot it in your own fiction. That step is the ability to see the rule violated in other people's fiction.

Once telling errors (and any other fiction craftsmanship errors) begin standing out to you like blinking lights in someone else's novel, you'll be on your way to achieving the ability to see them in your own fiction.

Just beware: If you do successfully learn how to see fiction errors in others' writing, you may no longer respect those writers' work. I've had more than a few novelists drop off my favorites list when I've gone back to their work and seen them violating many of the rules I consider necessary for good fiction.

It's like anything else: The more you learn what excellence looks like, whether it's in a golf swing or musicianship or computer programming, the less tolerant you'll be of mediocrity. It's the price of growing in your own skill.

SPOT THE TELLING

Now we're going to play a game of spot the telling. To give you practice at spotting telling in someone else's fiction, I'm giving you a few passages of text I've written myself. See if you can spot the telling in these five examples.

EXAMPLE 1

Jenny had always loved spring. It was a season of new life and new beginnings. She often remarked to her friend, Louise, as they would walk their dogs to the park, that spring was a new chance to do the year right. This time, she always told herself, this time I won't mess up my life. This year will be different.

EXAMPLE 2

"No, Wiggles!"

Jenny pulled her poodle away from the baby sitting on the picnic blanket.

The blanket was a red-and-white check that reminded her of the blanket she and Jerome had sat on during their first date. The clouds had blown in as if expecting something interesting to happen and were crowding together to get a look. Unfortunately the cloud cluster had resulted in a cloudburst, and she'd almost lost her chance with Jerome.

"Come, Wiggles. Bad dog."

EXAMPLE 3

Jenny sat on the park bench, her former high-hurdles championship legs no longer what they used to be. The leader of the local moms-and-tots group at Hilltop Church tied her dog's leash to the bench and opened her magazine. The plump mother of six crossed her ankles and tried to forget that tomorrow she would meet up with Jerome, her ex-boyfriend who, twenty years ago, had dumped her after the high school prom.

EXAMPLE 4

"Hello, Jenny."

Jenny looked up at the sound of her name. It was a man's voice that had spoken. She shielded her eyes against the sun, which was right at the man's shoulder and thus shining into her eyes. His was a trim and muscular silhouette.

"I'm sorry." Jenny started with an apology because when she was a child she learned she could make things better by making them her fault. "So sorry. I can't see you. Who am I talking with?"

EXAMPLE 5

The man seemed to hesitate a moment, standing still with the advantage on his side. Then he stepped to the right so Jenny could see him.

Jerome.

He looked amazing. In high school he'd been painfully thin but still handsome. Now he'd certainly filled out. His eyes were that same piercing blue, and his hair, that silken curtain of blond, still called to her to touch and fix. Her eyes went straight to his left hand. No ring.

Of course, *her* left hand did have one. She slid that hand under her thigh and wished she could instantly drop three dress sizes.

"Hello, Jerome."

He smiled that same crooked grin. "Hello, gorgeous."

ANSWER KEY

Could you spot the telling? There's a trick in there, so be sure you really can see it. Don't read the answers until you're sure.

Example 1 is all telling. Absolutely nothing happens. If it were a movie, it would've been the equivalent of sixty seconds of blank screen. That's bad.

In example 2 the telling begins in the second half of the first sentence in the third paragraph. In other words, everything in that paragraph after "The blanket was a red-and-white check … ." Did you see it? It's backstory, maybe even a flashback, and it definitely stops the story.

Example 3 contains what I call sneaky telling. The passage doesn't stop to include whole paragraphs of telling; little bits of it get slipped in as we go. If this were a movie, how in the world could the viewer know she was a former hurdles jumper, she was about to meet her boyfriend, or she had six children? The viewer couldn't. That information was not conveyed through scene, action, or dialogue. It was spoon-fed by means of telling. The writer cheated. Sneaky telling.

The telling in example 4 is harder to spot, but it's there. Did you see it? It's where the author explains Jenny's motivation for apologizing ("Jenny started with an apology because …").

Example 5 is the trick. There is no telling in it. Description, yes, but that's not telling, as we've seen.

Technically this might be telling: "In high school he'd been painfully thin but still handsome. Now he'd certainly filled out." In the sense of backstory, that could be telling. But it's description because it's contrasting how he looks now with how he looked in her memory.

Description is not the same thing as telling. You need description to further the story. You don't need telling at all. And her thoughts (wishing to drop three dress sizes) are not telling, either, at least not by my definition.

Be sure that, in your zeal to trim the telling, you don't also throw out things it's okay to include. Character thoughts (as long as they don't go into exposition and backstory) and description of setting, character, and action, are not telling. They're needed.

NEED TO GO THROUGH THE EXERCISE AGAIN?

Well, how'd you do? Hopefully this has been part of a learning process for you, especially if you weren't able to automatically see the telling in those examples. Keep looking at them until they pop out at you. Then turn to other fiction on your shelf and read it with a critical eye. You'll begin to see it, believe me.

That's a good thing, even if it spoils your regard for certain authors. Seeing the telling in other people's fiction is the prerequisite to being able to see it in yours. And seeing it in yours is the prerequisite to cutting it from yours, which may well be the prerequisite to getting published.

chapter 30

WHEN CAN READERS BEAR EXPOSITION?

Writing fiction should not be mechanical or formulaic. However, there are some formulas or rules of thumb that can help the novelist out.

As you know by now, I don't like telling. I don't like telling as exposition, telling as backstory, or telling to explain everyone's motivations. I don't like flashbacks, and I don't like recaps. I don't even like "Oh, I'm so glad you asked" conversations, which I call *telling in quotation marks.*

Telling, in my view, is bad because it stops the story and forces the reader to receive information she doesn't care about. However, telling can be useful, and there are circumstances where it can be used effectively.

In my Operation: Firebrand novels I invariably have a briefing scene in which someone informs the characters, and thus the reader, what's going on and what has to happen in the story. Someone stands up and gives an information dump. Isn't that telling?

In this case, no. Here's why.

Read what I wrote a few paragraphs back. Telling stops the story and forces unwanted information onto the reader like a commercial you can't mute. In my Firebrand novels, the briefing scene doesn't stop the story. Indeed, the story simply *can't go forward without it.* Nor does it force the reader to wade through boring information. The reader is interested in what's going to be covered.

Those are the two conditions for including (what seems to be) telling in the story: The information must be required for the story to go forward, and the reader must be interested in hearing it. Here it is as a formula: Your reader can tolerate telling to the degree she is interested in what is being told and to the degree the story can't advance without the information.

Let's say you've got a character who plays pro football. We're interested in his life and challenges. But then you launch into the story of his childhood. This doesn't work because we don't care about his childhood. So it's telling because you're stopping the story to tell us things we don't care about and without which the story could proceed.

But what if our player had been injured just before the big game, and you have the doctor come in and tell him what the prognosis and treatment plan is. The doctor's report—which is, it would seem, pure telling, because it's just an information dump—is not telling at all, because (1) the reader wants to know *and* (2) the story can't go on until we learn this information.

DEPOSITS AND WITHDRAWALS

Your reader will tolerate telling to the precise degree you've built up interest with her. Think of it as a bank account. If you give us zero deposits into our "interest account" on a given topic and then try to make a massive withdrawal (by making us listen to exposition on that topic, about which we have zero interest), you'll be instantly overdrawn, and you'll get nasty letters from your banker. Or, in this case, you'll get the disinterest of your reader.

Ah, but if you've made numerous deposits into that interest account, and now you want to tell us a little about it (but be sure it's something we must know to advance the story), go ahead and make that withdrawal. Build up our interest on a topic first. Then you can write a check on it—so long as it isn't for an amount larger than our "interest balance."

But be careful: You might have deposited three units of interest into that account, but if you try to withdraw an amount of telling that requires four or more, you'll be overdrawn again. You can blow the whole amount you've built up simply by lingering too long in telling mode.

A good example of this formula done right is in *Star Wars: Episode I*. We have lots of action and adventure in the movie before we ever have a long exposition scene. That's a good pattern to follow. (Don't start your story with telling, in other words.) Then, fairly deep into the movie, we do get one scene in which Anakin has taken Qui-Gon, Jar-Jar, and Padme to his house so his mother can make Jawa Root Salad. And they talk.

If you watch that scene carefully, you'll notice they're basically talking about what needs to happen, what they're going to do, and why they can't do it in other ways. It's an information dump—telling. And normally it would be a momentum killer. But it plays out fine—*and* we get our bearings about what's going to happen for the next hour of the movie.

There are a number of reasons why this works. First, it's a fairly interesting scene to watch. Qui-Gon catching Jar-Jar's tongue is a classic moment. There are also interesting interpersonal dynamics going on, like Anakin trying to get his mom to let him race again and Qui-Gon starting to put his Jedi moves on Anakin's mom. So it's not just exposition alone.

Second, we're interested. That's one of the conditions for a scene of telling to be okay in your book. How are our heroes going to get off this planet? How is this pure-hearted boy who loves his mom ever going to become Darth Vader? Why do we think Padme is more than she seems? The writer has built up enough viewer interest in this moment that we can bear the telling.

Third, the story simply can't proceed without this information. That's the other condition in our formula. The characters are stuck. But in this scene they come up with a plan for how to move forward.

The fourth reason this works is that this scene comes pretty deep into the story. The writer didn't try to give it to us within the first ten minutes of the movie. We're fully engaged in the story before the information dump comes. Lots of aspiring novelists I work with like to explain everything within the first twenty pages, feeling, perhaps, once all of that explanation is out of the way they can get on with the story.

But the *Star Wars* scene works. The formula is honored, and the exposition is successfully communicated.

Same with the briefing scenes in my Firebrand novels. The reader has become engaged in the plight of the people in danger, and she wants to know how and when the team is going to get there to save them. The interest level is high, and the story can't advance without this information.

LOOK INWARD

Analyze your story. Are you asking your reader to stomach large (or even small) quantities of telling about something in which she has zero interest? And I mean *story* interest here. A reader might be inherently interested in the inner workings of the internal combustion engine—but she might not be. You can't assume your reader will automatically be interested in something just because you put it in a book. You have to *make* the reader interested in the subject by making it important and interesting inside your story.

Chances are that the people who enjoyed *Operation: Firebrand—Crusade* were not, before they read my book, terribly interested in the plight of Christians in Sudan. But it was my job as a novelist to get the reader to invest in a character so she would begin to care. When the time came for the briefing, the reader's interest was quite high.

This is how techno-thrillers work, incidentally. And historical novels, for that matter. They educate as they entertain. But the education can't start until the entertainment is in high gear.

You can use almost all categories of telling—backstory, exposition, and character motivations—if you stick to this formula. Make sure you deposit in your reader interest bank (i.e., you engage your reader in this information) and that you make it so the reader must know this information for the story to proceed.

chapter 31
THE DUMB-PUPPET TRICK

Years ago I wrote puppet scripts for my church's children's department. Puppetry, like fiction, is a great way to have audience members or readers actually consider words of truth they probably wouldn't accept if preached from a pastor or written in a nonfiction book.

Often in these puppet scripts I would need to have some information come out to the audience, whether it be an explanation of what's going on, clarification of the plot points, or enunciation of the message. So I would bring in the dumb puppet.

> "Sally, why are you stacking up those Bibles? Are you going to start 'standing on the promises'? Gu-huh, gu-huh, gu-huh."
>
> "No, Jimmy! We're stacking these up because Leroy is going to give them away to the children during Backyard Bible Club next week."
>
> "Oh, so they can stand on the promises."
>
> "Well, in a way."
>
> "Because they're all short and can't see?"
>
> "No, Jimmy! So they can learn about Jesus and maybe become Christians."

If you'd had Sally talking to Leroy instead of to Jimmy (a.k.a. the dumb puppet), it wouldn't have worked. You can't have characters talk to each other about the details of things they both perfectly understand: the dreaded, "As you know, Bob …" error.

> "Wow, Leroy, I hope all these Bibles will be enough."
>
> "I do, too, Sally, because as you know we're going to be giving these out to the kids at BBC next week."
>
> "Yes, I do know that, Leroy. And as you know it is our hope that these kids will learn about Jesus and become Christians through these Bibles."

> "Exactly, Sally. Well said."

I mean, come on. Nobody talks like that. It's pure exposition you've tried to disguise by having characters utter it for no good reason.

But bring in the dumb puppet, and everything you need to have the audience know can get brought out in a believable way.

THE DUMB PUPPET IN FICTION

The dumb-puppet trick is very useful to bring out information in fiction. It helps you avoid exposition or backstory and prevents the Sally-and-Leroy kind of conversation in which everybody is talking about what they already know.

You could write:

> Jennifer had always loved interior decorating. It all started in 1973 when her mother had decided to redecorate the living room and kitchen of their ranch home in Southern California after the divorce.

You could also write:

> "Jennifer, I see that you love interior decorating."
>
> "Yes, Barb, I do."
>
> "I imagine it goes back to 1973 when your mother got divorced and decided to redecorate the kitchen and living room."
>
> "Yes, Barb, it does. How you know me."

Or you could let the dumb puppet save the day:

> "Jennifer, this room is lovely. I'm quite sure our readers will adore it."
>
> "Thank you, Sylvia. That's kind of you to say. I'm still in shock that your magazine wants to feature my work. I'm nobody."
>
> "Well, our editor doesn't think so." Sylvia looked down at her notepad. "So, when did you know you wanted to get into interior design?"

And you're off to the races.

Note that a dumb puppet doesn't have to be dumb. The reporter in the example above was quite intelligent. The thing that makes a dumb puppet isn't a low IQ, it's that he *doesn't already know what's going on.*

The dumb puppet is simply someone who is new to the situation and doesn't know all the whats and whys of the moment. He therefore has reason to ask about them. It is the asking (and the answering) that provides the natural way to convert information dumps into scenes of showing.

The next time you're going through your novel, and you see large chunks of exposition or backstory, and you're sure it's information that must be revealed to the reader, consider how you might bring in someone who could ask the right questions to bring it out organically.

Remember, anyone can be a dumb puppet—even a genius. The only qualification is that he or she (or *it,* for those who write speculative fiction) does not know the situation and might be reasonably expected to ask.

Children are great for this because they ask what no one else will. Visitors, tourists, reporters, the new guy, the visiting relative, the repairman, the inspector, and the deliveryman are all good candidates. Anyone who might have reason to ask things the reader needs to know.

The movie *Twister* has a feature-length dumb puppet. And the character serving this purpose is quite smart. *Twister* features a team of geeky scientists who chase tornadoes. They've all known each other for years. They speak their own storm-chaser geek lingo, which an outsider (like, say, the viewer) would have no clue how to interpret. So the writers turned to the dumb puppet.

Enter Dr. Melissa Reeves, the hero's new fiancée and a wonderful dumb puppet. Events in the story cause the good doctor to be swept along with these storm chasers as they do their geeky thing. They're constantly using terminology and high-tech equipment Melissa has never heard of before. This causes her to ask what it means and what it's for.

This is instant justification for something to be explained to the viewer. "Well, doc, we call this a mobile Doppler radar, and it … "

The dump puppet is your friend.

THE ARGUMENT OR THE BREAKDOWN

There's a variant to the dumb-puppet trick I'd like to tell you about.

As we've just seen, one situation in which people talk about things they already know is when there's a newcomer to the situation to whom it must be explained. As in *Twister.*

Another time people talk about things they all already know is when something goes wrong.

> "Why are you adding coolant to the asponerator? I told you never to do that."
>
> "I know what you told me, but look at the heat meter. It's maxed out. Your 'repairs' must've broken something else. Again."
>
> "Enough with that already. I fixed it, didn't I? And I know I didn't break anything this time. Maybe the meter's wrong."
>
> "It's not wrong. I ran a diagnostic. Maybe it's that new enzymer Keely put in."
>
> "Do you think it could be the strain? With five of us on the station now instead of three? Maybe it can't keep up? Maybe we're in trouble."

And so it goes. These two characters never would've talked about this had something not gone wrong.

Another variant of the dumb-puppet trick is the argument, which was also shown in the scene above. When people argue, especially when they're trying to assign blame, they talk about things they would normally leave unspoken:

> "You said you were going to pick her up at school."
>
> "When did I say that?"
>
> "This morning right after you spilled your coffee. Again."
>
> "Oh, so now with the personal attacks? Well, who's the one who ..."

Either an argument or a problem—or even both—can give you great freedom in bringing out information in a natural, organic way.

Use the dumb-puppet trick and its variants to convert your telling into showing.

With that, "Focus on the Craft: Showing vs. Telling" has come to its end. Now you are fully equipped to go hunting for telling in your manuscript and root it out.

Focus on the Craft:
POINT OF VIEW

After telling, the biggest thing that marks an amateur novelist, in my opinion, is point-of-view trouble.

Agents and acquisitions editors can see, usually on the first page, if an author has mastered point of view (POV). And if she hasn't, it's usually an easy way for the reviewer to know this person isn't yet ready for prime time.

So put your work gloves on, and let's dig into POV.

chapter 32

WHAT IS POINT OF VIEW?

Ah, point of view, that slayer of otherwise publishable manuscripts, that archfoe of the aspiring novelist.

POV is whose head we're in at any point in a novel. Whose eyes are we seeing through?

In the sentence "James looked both ways and crossed the street, careful to favor his gimpy ankle as he stepped," we're in James's head.

For the first part of the sentence we could've been looking through the eyes of someone else who was observing James, but when we got to that insight about his bum ankle, it clued us in that we were hearing a bit of James's thoughts. And that told us that we were inside James's POV.

Point of view is a bugaboo for many aspiring novelists. Besides *telling*, POV errors are the single most common problem I see in unpublished fiction manuscripts. I see POV problems in many published books, too.

The classic POV error is what is often called head-hopping. Instead of staying inside one character's head per scene, the author jumps around into multiple characters' viewpoints, giving us everyone's thoughts and interpretations.

It's akin to telling. It's much easier to just hop over to Susie's head and *tell* us what she's thinking than it is to *show* us what she's thinking by finding actions or words that might illustrate her inner state.

Head-hopping, like telling, is often the result of lazy, undisciplined writing, whereas a limited POV and scenes of showing are the path of discipline and excellence.

However, it's not technically incorrect. If you like to read fiction like this, or if it just doesn't bother you, then go for it in your own fiction. But many gatekeepers along the way may tell you that it's verboten. It's not (well, it might be at that gatekeeper's location), but it's sometimes seen as an error.

Head-hopping actually used to be the norm in English literature. It's called omniscient POV (because we know what everyone is thinking) and some best-selling novelists use it even today. Despite these precedents, omniscient may not be the point of view you should use for your fiction.

Let's look at the various forms of POV.

OMNISCIENT POV

In omniscient POV, as I've said, the novelist hops from head to head to tell us exactly what everyone is thinking and feeling. We never miss anything. We're given a God's-eye view of the whole situation.

Strictly speaking, omniscient POV is not an error. It is a legitimate way of handling point of view in fiction. Many successful authors use it today, and it was the viewpoint of choice in previous generations of fiction. My beloved J.R.R. Tolkien uses it some in *The Lord of the Rings*.

Here's an example of omniscient:

> "That's marvelous," Lucy said, thinking she could maybe parley this into a date, after all.
>
> Johnny noticed her thoughtful look and felt she must be thinking of trying to get as far away from him as possible. "Yeah, it's pretty cool."
>
> "You two are something else," Carlotta said, fearing that her chances with Johnny might be drying up. She had to do something drastic. "Hey, Johnny, come here a minute. I want to ask you something."
>
> *Oh, great,* Johnny thought. *Here it finally comes.* "Why don't you tell me from there?"

Can you see it? Do you notice you are privy to every person's thoughts? That's omniscient POV.

Like I said, there's nothing technically wrong with that. It's just lazy. In fact, it's a whole lot like telling. Maybe it *is* telling in another form. It's also less realistic. Your reader is most probably not omniscient in real life. She is more likely accustomed to knowing only what she knows and trying to use clues to discern what everyone else is thinking and feeling.

If you want your reader to identify with your protagonist, let her get close *to that character only* by letting her be privy to only that character's thoughts, feelings, and perceptions.

It's counterintuitive. You'd think letting your reader in on everyone's thoughts would create intimacy with all characters equally. But it doesn't work that way. It actually creates equal distance from all of them because the reader doesn't know who to pull for or get close to.

In the name of intimacy, omniscient POV creates distance. It's strange but true that the real way to create intimacy is to *not* give the reader access to everyone's thoughts. You must stay limited to one viewpoint character per scene if you want to create a connection between the reader and the POV character.

Finally, omniscient POV is discouraged because it removes the mystery from your characters and deprives you of the ability to surprise your reader. How can you conceal who the bad guy is if you've been giving us his nefarious thoughts all along? How can you keep the reader in suspense over whether John Black can be trusted if you've allowed us to hear that he's wholeheartedly on the hero's side? How can you keep us guessing about Julie's true affections if we've been hearing them from page one?

When it comes to suspense and character intrigue, omniscient POV is about as subtle as a stampeding elephant.

Omniscient POV is like abstract art. Sure, anyone can slosh paint on a canvas and call it "Woman in a Hat," but only someone with extensive art theory training can actually make it work. In the same way, it takes a grand master of fiction to pull off a novel in omniscient POV. Anyone can hop around into every character's head and call it omniscient, but without mastering the other disciplines of fiction it will probably feel like a hack job.

My advice: Consider avoiding omniscient POV until *Publishers Weekly* refers to you as a grand master of fiction.

THIRD-PERSON POV

Third person is the most common POV style used in modern fiction.

There are books about fiction out there that subdivide third person into third-person limited, third-person objective, third-person omniscient, etc. But for my purposes, we'll just call it third person and be done with it.

Third person is the he-said/she-said style of point of view. Here's an example of third person as I define it:

> "That's a lovely hat, Meredith." In truth, Tom thought the hat was ridiculous, but now wasn't the time for candor.
>
> "Why, thank you, Tommy," Meredith said, looking shy. "You don't think it's too much, do you?"
>
> "Oh, no! Of course not. Not for you."
>
> Her face clouded. Uh-oh. What had he said? Her eyes narrowed. "You're not just saying that because you want to get close to me, are you? I never could read you, Tommy."
>
> "Um … "
>
> "Never mind. I prefer not knowing."

You see it, right? We get Tom's thoughts but not Meredith's. We see Meredith's face cloud (as if we're looking at her through Tom's eyes) but we don't know for sure what it means, because *Tom* doesn't know what it means. He can only guess, and the guessing tells us as much about Tom as about Meredith.

This restrictiveness and uncertainty feel more realistic because it's how we perceive the world, too. Third person also allows you to keep characters' true motives and loyalties hidden, something the novelist needs to do often.

In third person, you have one viewpoint character per scene. Think of it as a periscope on a submarine. There are multiple crewmen on the sub, but only one gets to look into the world above the surface. That one crewman, staring through the eyepiece and describing what he sees, is the viewpoint character for the whole sub. So it is with fiction: In each scene, pick one character to be the one through whose eyes we witness the action.

You can change viewpoint characters in subsequent scenes. You're not locked into one for the whole book (unless you choose to do it that way). But once a scene begins, you *are* locked into that character's head. So choose wisely.

In third person, you are limited to what the viewpoint character can see, hear, and know. If the viewpoint character can't see or know something that's happening in the scene, you can't tell the reader about that thing. Remember the periscope idea. If something happens outside the view of the periscope, no one in the sub can know about it. You can't show us something the periscope can't detect.

The kind of discipline that comes from limiting your perceptions and choosing POV characters will reap benefits for you in all areas of your fiction mastery.

Another restriction of third-person POV concerns the element of thought: The viewpoint character can't know things she shouldn't know. So when a stranger walks into the room—even if it's someone the reader recognizes from other scenes—if the viewpoint character doesn't know this stranger, she can't refer to her by her name. That would be a POV violation. The viewpoint character couldn't know it, so we can't know it either.

Third person is the best choice for most novelists and most novels. I recommend you write just about everything in third person until you've got a couple novels under your belt.

FIRST-PERSON POV

First person is the most intimate POV there is. This is the "I" and "me" POV. With first person, you're so close to the viewpoint character there is no distance between you and her.

Here's an example:

> "Lois, why did you buy that?" I figured I knew why, but I thought I'd best check.
>
> She looked annoyed at my question. "I needed it for work. I told you about the presentation, remember, or weren't you listening?"
>
> Next she'll attack my video game hobby. "Oh, okay."
>
> "I don't know why you hassle me about these things. What was that memory card thingie you bought for your console last week? You didn't tell me about that. You just showed up with it."
>
> Called it.

With first person you're so close to the viewpoint character's thoughts you're essentially one with him. The vocabulary you use in these scenes ought to sound like the thoughts, words, and phrases he would use. First person is the Vulcan Mind Meld of fiction.

A great time to choose first person is when you're writing about someone very different and distant from your typical reader, but to whom you want that reader to feel close.

For instance, in *Operation: Firebrand—Deliverance* I chose first-person POV for the scenes where I was seeing through the eyes of a pregnant North Korean woman. Talk about someone who was different from my reader—not to mention from me! But I wanted the reader to span the distance and understand how familiar and *normal* she was. I wanted the reader to care about her more than anyone else in the book. So she was the character I chose to write in first-person POV. I let her be the "I" and "me" of the book, which meant she would be the character the reader felt closest to.

With first person what you lose in objectivity (compared to third person) you gain in intimacy with the viewpoint character.

First person is also great when you want to create a claustrophobia—a claustrophobia similar to what your detective protagonist is feeling, perhaps—because you're stuck inside only one person's head. If you want the reader to feel isolated and insulated and kind of blind to what's going on beyond just the protagonist's immediate surroundings (like in a suspense thriller in which no one can be trusted), first person is for you. It's also great when you just want to create intense reader-hero intimacy and bonding.

Like third person, first person is limited to what the viewpoint character can see, hear, and know. If he doesn't see, hear, or know it, neither can the reader. This takes discipline but is well worth your effort.

First person is the second most common POV used in modern fiction. Try your hand at it. It's wonderful.

CINEMATIC POV

I think I've just made this term up. As far as I know, it's not a legitimate style of POV. I wanted a way to describe what I've seen in some unpublished manuscripts.

In this style, the author zooms in on every character's reactions or actions but does not give us his or her thoughts. It's like a camera that sees all, even if the viewpoint character can't see it. It's like head-hopping because we're privy to what everyone is doing even if no one viewpoint character could see them all, but it's not truly omniscient POV, because we don't know what everyone is thinking.

For example:

> Jimmy tied his shoes and resumed his walk to school.
>
> Behind the bushes, a predator lurked. It tracked Jimmy's progress with its eyes.
>
> Inside the house, Mrs. Tucker washed dishes and rubbed her temples. She looked like she needed a power nap.
>
> The mailman rounded the corner and pulled up to the first mailbox. Today he wore those funny postman shorts.

Whose head are we in here? No one's. We're in the author's head, I suppose. We see everything, but externally. We don't know anyone's thoughts. We're on the outside of everyone. But we don't miss anything.

This strange, distant-spectator POV is cropping up here and there in the manuscripts I've seen. It makes sense, I guess, so much of modern fiction is more like a movie than traditional fiction. Maybe things are moving in that direction.

But I don't like it. Fiction still does do a few things better than movies can do, and getting the viewpoint character's thoughts and feelings is one of them. I would hate to be limited for a whole book to only what an external "camera" observer could see.

MIXING POVS

Finally, let's talk about using different POV styles within the same book.

In my first three novels I used third person exclusively. Then in my second three novels I used a mixture of third person and first person.

How do you mix POV styles? I did it by choosing one character to be my first-person viewpoint character and using third person for all the other viewpoint characters. I chose one person to feature, if you will, and used first person for that character. In a sense, it was that person's book. Every other viewpoint character in the story just got the third-person treatment.

If your novel has only one viewpoint character, you're golden. Just pick third or first person and stick with it throughout. But if you've got more than one viewpoint character, consider doing one in first person and the rest in third.

One warning: Don't do more than one first-person viewpoint character in the same book. It's confusing to the reader. "Now which 'I' am I with now?" Pick one viewpoint character to bring your reader closest to. Do the rest in third person.

chapter 33
SPOT THE POV ERROR

The second portion of our section on POV is a game of spot the POV error. This is a great intermediate step to learning how to spot errors in your own fiction—which is notoriously hard to do. So let's play a version of the game to help you learn to see POV errors in your own fiction.

The premise we're working under is that it's all but impossible to go from head knowledge to practical application when it comes to the "rules" of fiction. It's one thing to know one of those rules. It's something else entirely to see where you've violated that rule in your own writing.

As I mentioned in the previous chapter, what's called omniscient POV is not technically an error. It's simply another style of POV. But it's so often used by writers whose fiction skill set is low, and it's so closely associated to telling, that to me it *is* an error. So I'll treat it as such in one or more of the examples that follow.

SPOT THE POV ERROR

So let's play.

EXAMPLE 1

"Surprise! I'm home!"

Jimmy reacted in horror. What was Tom doing home now? It wasn't even July yet. "Uh, hi, Tom."

The news caught Connie by surprise, too, but for a different reason. She thought he wasn't going to announce his arrival. They were supposed to meet outside town and then seem to arrive together. "Tom," she said with her eyes narrowed, "this is … unexpected."

Tom couldn't believe their reactions. "Aren't you guys glad to see me?"

EXAMPLE 2

Connor was tired. The spry warrior of yesteryear stretched his feet out on the couch. How did it come to this? His emerald eyes glistened as he thought of his buddies lost in the war. One, in particular. His face clouded as the image of Kane's broken body flashed across his mind.

EXAMPLE 3

Clete hauled the last hay bale into the barn. He came into the yard rubbing his lower back. A man stood beside the bulldozer blade, a hiker's backpack high on his back.

"Can I help you, stranger?" Clete said. Where was that worthless dog, anyway?

The stranger raised a hand against the hot Kansas sun. "I'm looking for a particular farm."

Clete heard a deep Southern accent in the man's voice. Maybe he was good folk after all. "Which one?"

Davis O'Bannon removed the backpack from his shoulders and leaned it against the wood fence. "Family farm. Name of Oldfield."

Clete nodded. The Oldfields had come from somewhere down south. "'Bout a mile east of here, off of Farm to Market Road two-nine-five." He rubbed his back again. "You want a drink or something? Iced tea, maybe?" Didn't all Southerners like iced tea?

Davis smiled with perfect teeth. "Much obliged."

EXAMPLE 4

The blond waitress looked at the customer like he was a roach. "You've got a real sense of humor, don't you?"

The former gunnery sergeant just laughed. "I guess not."

"It's hard to be really funny, isn't it?" she asked, swallowing hard.

He looked down at the menu. "I wouldn't know."

EXAMPLE 5

Doyle and Dexter entered the hotel lobby at precisely eleven thirty. Doyle swept his eyes across the pink marble flag-

> stones and the ornate chandelier, conscious of Dexter's open-mouthed expression. The boy could be such a yokel. He could use that.
>
> "Come," the older man said, "let's check in."
>
> "Sounds good to me," Dexter said, smelling chlorine. "And then I'm hitting the pool."

ANSWER KEY

Did you see them? There's some crossover with *spot the telling*, too. Did you notice that? Telling and POV errors often go together in fiction not ready for publication.

So let's see how you did.

Example 1 is simply omniscient POV. We get everyone's thoughts and feelings. It's classic "head-hopping." The whole thing is a POV error.

In example 2 we're inside Connor's mind. We find out he's tired, and we are privy to what he thinks and remembers. How, then, can we know that his emerald eyes glistened or his face clouded? Does he happen to be looking into the mirror the moment he thinks this? Probably not. This is an observation by an external (i.e., non-Connor) person, which makes it a POV error.

Did you catch the part that is also a bit of sneaky telling? "The spry warrior of yesteryear." Is he really thinking this about himself? Did he think, *Ah, me, it's good to be a spry warrior of yesteryear and stretch my feet out on the couch?* Not likely. Which makes that a POV error, too. And telling.

When you've got POV under your belt, the POV violation in example 3 will hit you like a pitcher of ice water. Did you see it?

The Southern man with the backpack is a stranger to Clete. So how do we suddenly learn that the man's name is Davis O'Bannon? If Clete hadn't just learned the man's name (as through an introduction in the scene or the like), and Clete is our viewpoint character, how can *we* suddenly know the stranger's name? We can't. That's a blatant POV violation.

Do you see how this is related to telling? The author (well, in this case, *me*) was afraid you wouldn't get who this guy was, so he told you his name. Plus, *I* knew who the stranger was, so maybe I just let it slip out without realizing I'd made an error. Or maybe I wanted to be sure you got it, so I jumped heads.

It didn't come out through dialogue, though it easily could've. It was simply given to you. The author violated the restrictions of POV and spoon-fed you the information.

If you give information to the reader the viewpoint character couldn't know, you've committed a POV error. And probably telling, as well.

There are exceptions, such as when you let the reader figure something out that the viewpoint character doesn't know. For instance, if we had had forty pages in Davis O'Bannon's viewpoint and had known that he always took his backpack off when talking to strangers, then when this interloper on Clete's farm takes his backpack off, we'll know it's Davis O'Bannon, even though the viewpoint character doesn't know that, and the author hasn't violated Clete's POV.

Most of the time, though, if the POV character doesn't know or detect something, the reader can't know or detect it, either.

Example 4 is tricky. You probably noticed the sneaky telling: "the former gunnery sergeant." That's akin to "the spry warrior of yesteryear" in example 2.

The other problem with this example is that you don't really know whose head you're in. Maybe you're in the customer's viewpoint because he might describe the waitress as blonde, whereas she wouldn't sit around thinking of herself as the blonde waitress.

But later we learn that the waitress swallowed hard, which sounds like something only she would know. And then we learn that the customer is a former gunnery sergeant. Well, does she know this about him? It's telling, but at least it might be something she would know. Except that he seems to be a stranger to her ("the customer"), so how would she know he used to be in the military?

This is another case of omniscient POV. The writer has not exercised the self-discipline to restrict himself to the thoughts, senses, and interpretations of the viewpoint character. The irony is that this distances the reader every time, though the author thinks he's bringing the reader closer because he's revealing everyone's thoughts.

In example 5, the first POV error comes in the phrase "the older man." We're clearly in Doyle's POV in this scene. He looks around the lobby, and we get to see what he sees. He thinks of Dexter as "the boy." All well and good. But then suddenly we see Doyle described as "the older man." Well, he's obviously older if he thinks of Dexter as a boy. But who thinks this thought? Does he describe himself as "the older man"?

This isn't a hop over to Dexter's head; it's just a violation of Doyle's perspective. It's not something he would think or detect, and yet it's given to us on a platter. That violation of perspective makes it a POV error.

Finally, we do jump over to Dexter's POV when we learn that he smells chlorine. If the POV character (in this case, Doyle) can't sense or know it, the reader can't learn about it. Stay disciplined. Stay inside one head per scene.

Keep reading those examples until you can see the shifts instantly. Then begin spotting them in the fiction you read.

When you can do that, you'll be ready to see these errors—or lack of them—in your own fiction.

chapter 34

ESTABLISH YOUR POV RIGHT AWAY

I'm a big believer in establishing things early in any given scene. Whether it's what the place looks like, who's there, what time of day it is, or whose head we're in, I like knowing right away.

There are reasons you'll occasionally want your reader to be left guessing about who the scene is about, where it's taking place, or what time of day it is. But most of the time you're going to want to let your reader know immediately what's going on.

In "Focus on the Craft: Description," I do a whole series on describing the setting of a scene. You'll notice there I urge you to give this descriptive information by the midpoint of the first page of any scene.

The same holds true with POV. Very early in a scene—in the very first line or two—you need to let us know whose head we're in. Whose eyes are we seeing through?

You should name or otherwise identify your viewpoint character in *the first sentence* of a new scene, if not the first word.

ORIENTEERING

Novelists don't always realize how disorienting it is to read a novel. They don't always understand how heavily readers rely on them to get them grounded in a scene and setting. But with the simple absence of certain elements (or, worse, the presence of misleading elements), the reader will become confused and frustrated.

For example:

> Jenny took the baby upstairs and put her in her crib. She sat in the rocker for a few minutes, just enjoying being a mommy. Larry watched her go and then decided to blow out of town and become a used-car salesman.

Confused?

If I did that right, you thought for two whole sentences that we were in Jenny's head. But then suddenly I reveal that I've supposedly been in Larry's head the whole time. Or maybe I was first in Jenny's head and then in Larry's. Either way, it's disorienting.

If we had stayed with Jenny and continued to give us Jenny's thoughts, it would've been a good way to start the scene. Right away you've told us whose eyes we're seeing through. Excellent.

But it didn't stay with Jenny. It jumped to Larry pretty early on, leading us to wonder if maybe we're in his head. It was confusing and off-putting.

Here's another example:

> The movie started late, though it was almost impossible to tell because of the new advertising-previews thingy they were showing now instead of the ad slide show of yore. It was annoying that people had brought young children to this R-rated movie. How selfish or careless were these so-called parents? The movie did start, finally, and it was enjoyable. The credits at the end were even entertaining. Ian almost hated to have to blow the place up.

Okay, we've been through an entire two-hour movie without knowing whose head we were in. Who thought the parents were selfish? We don't know. Who missed the ad slide show of yesteryear? We don't know. It's only at the end that we figure out whose head we're in.

And what if the last sentence had revealed the viewpoint character was really a kindly old retiree? That would change everything.

How we interpret a scene is based on whose eyes we're seeing it through. Keeping us in the dark about whose POV we're in is like telling us only at the end of a scene that all along it's supposedly been pouring down rain the whole time. If you don't tell us until the end, we don't receive it. In our minds, what you didn't tell us hasn't actually happened at all. We reject it.

Establish POV right away in every scene. Take a look at some scenes in your work-in-progress. Have you identified whose head we're in right away, like in the first sentence? If not, see if you can work that in there. It's okay to occasionally wait until the third line or so to establish this. Just be sure you're doing it intentionally and that you're not including misleading or confusing clues.

chapter 35

THE VIEWPOINT CHARACTER AS NARRATOR

The final element of point of view is what I consider an advanced technique. It's something every novelist ought to try to move toward. It feels artsy and very fun to do, and it will enrich your fiction.

AUTHOR AS NARRATOR VS. CHARACTER AS NARRATOR

Most novelists have a "narrator voice," a way of writing in the nondialogue passages of their books that doesn't sound like any character in the story. Rather, this narrator voice usually sounds most like the author's natural way of writing.

In virtually all of my fiction examples in this book, and in all of my regular text passages (like this one), you've heard Jeff Gerke's natural writing voice. That's my narrator voice. But in this chapter I'm going to ask you to take on the character of one of the people from your books and tell the story in his or her voice.

This isn't simply limiting yourself to one head per scene, though it certainly begins there. This isn't just including only your viewpoint character's thoughts or knowledge. This goes one step beyond so you're actually having the story told to you *by the character.*

Imagine hearing *Star Wars* from the perspective of Darth Vader. Or C-3PO. Or Lando Calrissian. What if one of those characters was your guide, your periscope? Can you feel how the whole experience would be flavored differently, depending on whose lens you're seeing it through?

That's what I'm talking about here. What if you conveyed your story not through narrator voice but through the voice of one of the characters in your book?

There's nothing technically wrong with having a characterless narrator voice, especially when using the third-person POV. All my books are done that way, as are most of the books from my peers. But I'm here to tell you about a level of mastery you may now be ready to attempt.

In this more enlightened method, you *use the viewpoint character as the narrator.*

DEEP COVER

Point of view is all about restricting yourself to the things the viewpoint character can see, hear, smell, taste, feel, and know. What the protagonist thinks, feels, assumes, senses, and says must come from the framework of the information he has access to.

Likewise, this person must speak in ways that are accurate and true to that character. Right? If the character holds a PhD in applied physics, you don't expect him to speak like a construction worker. His spoken dialogue must be consistent with his character.

If a character's dialogue must be true to his character, and if he must be restricted to what he could know, doesn't it make sense that this character's *interior* dialogue ought to be true to his character and restricted to what he could know? In other words, if this character sounds a certain way when speaking, shouldn't this character sound the same way when thinking?

And what is narration in a novel but an extension of what the viewpoint character is thinking?

If we're in this character's head for this scene, aren't we seeing it through his eyes? Aren't we getting it all through the filter of this character's personality, prejudices, and presuppositions?

THE GOSPEL TRUTH

Think about the four Gospels. Each covers the same story. Each is written either by an eyewitness or by someone who had access to eyewitnesses to the life, death, burial, and resurrection of Jesus Christ. And yet look how different all four of them are.

Matthew, Mark, and Luke are similar in many ways, but they also differ greatly. Matthew knows Christ's compassion. Mark loves the action scenes. And Luke is a stickler for historical detail. Then we've got John way out somewhere else doing his own thing.

They tell the same story, and yet they don't. They include different stories or bring out different emphases on the same stories. They speak to different audiences, they have different purposes, and they each leave you with a different message.

Here are four character-narrators giving us vastly different reading experiences because they're telling the same story through their own eyes, minds, and words.

So it should be in your fiction.

Not only should the stuff in quotation marks sound like your character, and not only should the character's thoughts sound like your viewpoint character, but the rest of it should sound like your viewpoint character, too. Look around where you are right now. Describe this setting—but do so in the words your viewpoint character would use. How would Indiana Jones describe a room differently from, say, Elle Woods in *Legally Blonde*? What would each of them notice? What vocabulary would they use? What commentary would they add? What conclusions would they draw?

Describe your setting from each of their points of view. Maybe do the exercise with two to four characters from your own book. Do it *in character*.

STAY IN CHARACTER

Instead of jumping out of everyone's character to adopt your generic writer voice for narration and description, stay in character. Use your viewpoint character's voice and personality to narrate and describe.

How would Hitler describe a room differently from how Gandhi would describe it? How would King Arthur describe an event differently from how Robin Hood would describe it? Rocky Balboa versus Rocky the Squirrel?

Here's a passage from my first novel, *Virtually Eliminated*, in which nine-year-old Jordan is narrating:

> Jordan knew he shouldn't get into a car with strangers, but these guys were FBI agents. Besides, the two agents—Ricky and Paul—seemed nice enough. They said they wanted to take him computer shopping. What could be wrong with that?
>
> And did they ever take him shopping! It was like Christmas, only he got to pick out all his own presents. They took him to a really nice computer store and told him to pick out

> the coolest stuff for net surfing. Everything—even a computer! They must've been rich because they didn't even blink when he picked out the most expensive computer in the store.
>
> They wouldn't let him buy any games, though. What was the use of this great machine if they weren't going to play with it?

There's a satisfactory description of the events as they unfolded, but you get it in the words of a nine-year-old computer-gaming freak. If I'd done it in *my* voice, it would've sounded more staid and therefore less interesting. Do this in your fiction, too.

YEAH, BUT YOU SAID ...

If you've read my online column, you may've read my tip on avoiding exclamation points in narration. And yet in that passage above, there were two. So which is it?

The answer is that the no-exclamation-points-in-narration rule applies when you're doing standard narration—when you're not attempting to put all your narration and description in the words and attitudes of your viewpoint character. When you're trying this advanced technique, you get more of a dialogue feel even in the narration, and in that case, exclamation points are fine.

ONLY I AM THE MASTER NOW

As you mature in your writing you are going to begin striving for the subtlety of a master craftsman. One way to approach that is to begin doing all your narration in character. If your viewpoint character uses exclamation points as part of how she thinks, by all means use them in narration.

Let your narration and description be an extension of your viewpoint character, and write it as that person would think and interpret it.

Note that you can do this even if you have multiple viewpoint characters in your book. Just make sure each character-narrator sounds like that character. Each scene from one viewpoint character ought to feel entirely different from scenes that come from another viewpoint character's perspective.

It will take discipline to adopt this new habit. You've probably learned very well how to jump in and out of a character's voice for dialogue and narration. Now I'm asking you to stay in character the whole time. That will take work. But it's worth it.

Every scene is told through the eyes and mind of a viewpoint character. You're already doing this, I hope. POV is one of the fundamental disciplines of writing fiction. Now add to that this level of artistry, and your fiction will continue its ascent to the level of mastery.

I hope you've gained some understanding of point of view as a crucial element of fiction craftsmanship. POV errors are one of those dealbreakers that can instantly kill your book's chances of being published. But agents and editors love reading the work of novelists who have mastered POV. It tells them the author has probably done the work in all levels of craftsmanship, and his book is to be considered seriously.

Focus on the Craft:

DESCRIPTION

As any of my Marcher Lord Press authors will tell you, I'm a stickler for description. The single most frequent note I give my authors in an edit is "I'm not picturing this setting; I'm getting no mental image here; please describe."

I am aware of the school of thought that says a novelist shouldn't describe anything. Readers, the thinking goes, ought to be allowed to form their own images of the places and people in the book. Far be it from the author to intrude on the reader's private virtual world by imposing his own interpretations of what things look like.

In my mind, a scene without good description is a scene the author left incomplete. Maybe the author was in a hurry or just didn't want to do the work of really picturing the setting, so he just left out that bit. Consequently, the reader doesn't get a mental picture of what the scene looks like, leaving it to take place in some vaporous haze of shifting gray cloud.

THE FULL WORKUP

Every setting in every scene in your book (and every character, too, by the way) must be fully described for the reader. If you're not seeing it, the reader sure won't be seeing it.

Remember, as they say in preaching: If it's a haze in the pulpit, it's a fog in the pew. Or as they say in theater: If it ain't on the page, it ain't on the stage.

In other words, if the writer doesn't imagine the setting himself and then render that description on the page, the reader will get nothing when she tries to imagine what's going on in the scene.

If the writer doesn't describe it, it doesn't exist for the reader. You may be picturing the setting perfectly (although maybe you're not), but if you don't write it down so the reader can peek over your shoulder, she gets zilch in terms of a sense for what's happening and where.

In my opinion, there are six main components to a full description of a setting:

- **Generic Descriptor:** Remember to let us know what the place is; these are words like *stadium, desert, closet,* and *cockpit.*

- **Establishing Shot:** With this part of the description you're answering the question "What am I looking at?" This is the big picture, the image you get when you paint with the wide brush. These are statements like "a vast clearing in the forest," "a crowded metropolis street at rush hour," and "an expensive-looking conference room that looked like it could seat thirty executives." Many novelists go straight to details like furniture or flowers but neglect to answer the most obvious question: "What is this place? What am I looking at here?"
- **Comparison:** Give us a word picture or simile to know what this place seems like, reminds the character of, or could be compared with; these are a terrific shorthand for the reader to get an instant handle on the setting. Use phrases like "the whole place reminded him of what the floor of a Chuck E. Cheese's must look like at closing time," "the pond wasn't any larger than the YMCA pool back home," or "the office looked like a cross between a factory floor and a powder room." Word pictures are your secret weapon for descriptions.
- **Lighting:** That's my catch-all term for whether the setting is indoor or outdoor, whether it's day or night (and, if daytime, about what time of day), and the weather (if it's outside). You might know that it's a dark and stormy night, but you'd be surprised how many times novelists leave out that kind of information—and its pretty significant for helping the reader picture the scene.
- **Detail:** This includes evocative bits that help sell the setting, like that odd piece of furniture or the antique violin on the table. It also includes the full sensory sweep: What do I hear, smell, taste, feel, and see in this setting?
- **Place the Players on the Stage:** How many people are here, what are they doing, and where are they in relation to one another? When you walk into a room, this is one of the first things you notice (massive crowd? only ten people? your mom and the janitor?), yet many novelists don't include this information, so we find out only at the end of the scene that really the entire cheerleading squad has been watching the whole thing. Place

> the players on the stage as soon as the scene begins so we can know what we would know if we were actually there.

That last phrase is the key. The goal of a description is to reveal for the reader everything she would notice in the first second of a scene if this were a movie. As soon as the picture comes on the screen and sound comes from the speakers, we get an instant gestalt of what we're looking at. We're instantly oriented. That's what you should be giving your reader with a description.

Now, not every setting needs the full workup with all six major components. If your character is passing down a hallway, for instance, you don't need to give the full workup of that setting. But you need to provide *something* so the reader can begin to imagine the place. And if anything significant happens in that setting, it had better receive the full treatment.

Don't get legalistic or formulaic about this. Some settings can really be helped by a description of the dominant aroma of the place, for instance, but we don't need to know what every setting smells like.

It's okay if you don't write descriptions while you're doing your first draft, by the way. Maybe you don't want to stop and describe it all, because you're in the midst of a creative fervor, and slowing down to write a description would scare away the muse. That's okay. But you'd better be sure you dedicate several days to combing back through your manuscript and including thorough descriptions for every setting in your book.

chapter 36

WHY DESCRIBE?

One of the most common complaints I have of beginning (and many advanced) novelists' fiction is I just can't imagine the scene. I don't know what anything looks like. I can't picture where I am or what's going on.

This is the fault of the writer. As a reader I *want* to fill in the blanks for the author. If you give me something to go on, I'll help you out with the rest. But you have to give me something, or I'm lost. And few things frustrate me more than not being able to figure out what's going on in a scene I'm reading.

Some authors feel it's a good idea to ration the description of the setting, doling it out here and there throughout the scene so that by the *end* of the scene, the reader finally knows what the place looks like. I hate that. I think what the author is trying to do is avoid the supposedly dreaded paragraph of nothing but description. Perhaps they feel that such a paragraph is *telling* and stops the story cold.

As we've seen, description is not telling. How else is the reader going to know what the place looks like if you don't describe it? Do you give us a weather report every time? No, unless it's pertinent. Do you give us a 360-degree panorama of every setting? No, unless it's important for us to know right now. But you *must* describe what the place looks like, or we won't know what we're seeing. We'll feel distanced from the story. Minds will begin to drift.

A scene without a detail-laden description of the setting is like one of those experimental theatrical productions with just gray geometric shapes on the stage. They're supposed to be *suggestive* rather than specific. It makes it easier on the set builders, too. Do you really want your scenes to feel like they're on a stage filled with gray blobs? Or, worse, to feel like there's no setting at all, just talking heads?

That's what you get when you have a dialogue scene with insufficient description. The lines of dialogue go back and forth without anything tying them to the ground. They begin to become detached from their tethers like hot-air balloons, floating up into a vague ether of gray nothingness. Stop and give us a paragraph of description. Find long dialogue passages and insert little tie-downs to the setting. (More on this in the discussion on beats in Chapter 42.)

Describe your setting very early in the scene. I stipulate that my authors begin describing the setting by at least the bottom of the first page of a new scene. Sometimes you can start a scene with a description, but very often you want to include some nondescriptive text—dialogue or action—to engage us in the scene. But by the bottom half of the first page of that new setting, you should be describing the setting, or your reader will be frustrated.

Note this applies every time you change locations—*even when you move from one setting to another within the same scene.* You always need to give us a paragraph of description of the new place. (By the by, this applies to characters, too. Be sure to describe them as soon as they step onstage.)

When a filmmaker turns on the camera, the viewer immediately knows a lot about where the action is, who's there, what everyone's doing, what time of day it is, and what everyone looks like. This is automatic with the director's toolkit. The author of fiction is not so lucky. She has to actually spell it all out, as do you.

chapter 37
THE ESTABLISHING SHOT

When you watch a movie, sometimes you see the skyline of a big city. Then there's a cut, and you see a closer shot of someone walking down a city street. When the shot switches from wide to tight, you understand that the person you see in the tight shot is placed somewhere in the setting you saw in the wide shot, right?

If you see an aerial shot of snowy mountains, and then you see a closer shot of a wizard and a Balrog fighting on a snowy mountainside, you assume this fight is taking place somewhere in that mountain range you saw in the first shot. You don't assume that first shot was mountain scenery the director liked, and the shot of the wizard and Balrog fighting is actually taking place in some other setting far away from those mountains.

If you see a blimp shot of a football stadium, and then you see a close shot of a couple huddled together in the stands, you assume they're at that stadium watching a game.

These wide shots are all examples of what filmmakers call "establishing shots." They *establish* for the viewer the wider, macro context of the action we're going to be watching at a more micro level. They give the reader a sense of *where* the action is taking place.

Even in movies or shows that pride themselves on not using establishing shots (like the TV series *Lost*) you still very quickly see the context of where things are happening: beach in the background, jungle all around, cave, hatch, etc. As soon as the camera comes on, the viewer understands where she is.

For the viewer to understand what's going on, the filmmaker must show him *where* it's going on. Two people having a swordfight is interesting, but devoid of context it's not as interesting (or meaningful) as it could be. Are they onstage in a play? Are they in the middle of a medieval melee? Are they on a crossbeam high above a pirate ship? The establishing shot gives meaning and placement to the action that will follow.

USE THESE IN YOUR FICTION

Establishing shots are not for movies only. In fiction, if your reader doesn't know *where* the action is taking place, she won't understand *what* is taking place.

Two people start talking. They're talking about important matters, but you have no clue where they are. Maybe you find out from the author that the characters are "outside." Well, what does that mean? Outside in the Bahamas or outside on the tundra of Kazakhstan? Is it night or day? Raining, snowing, cold, hot, windy, or fair? Are other people there, or are they alone? Is there traffic nearby? What are the characters wearing? What are they doing? Are they walking or working out or lazing on the grass? Are they at a park or in a dark alley?

One of the things that aggravates me most about some fiction I see is there is inadequate description of the location where any given scene is taking place. I hate not knowing where this is or what the people are doing. As a writer, it is *your job* to inform the reader what the context of your scenes is.

In film, the viewer gets a huge gestalt of the characters' setting just by looking at the screen. Even if there is no true establishing shot (like an aerial overview of the location) the viewer can still see behind the character to know a few things about where this is taking place, what time of day it is, who else is there, and so forth.

This benefit doesn't exist in fiction. The reader can't see behind your characters to fill in the setting. If you don't enlighten her as to what's there, it simply isn't there for her. Maybe they're in a spaceship, underwater, or in an office building. Maybe the characters are wearing hobo outfits, scuba gear, or Groucho Marx noses. The reader just doesn't know. And that's the writer's fault.

In your fiction, *whenever you put us in a new location*, you must give us a description of what the place looks like, how many people are there, what they're wearing, what they're doing, where they are in relation to one another, and anything else the reader needs to understand the moment.

You need to give us an establishing shot. Otherwise, we'll be lost. You don't have to be formulaic about it. You don't have to say, "Okay, first, are they inside or outside? Second, what does it look like? Third …" You don't have to give these descriptions on the first line of any new scene. Don't get locked into doing it one way.

But you must, very early in every new setting, tell us what it's like, who is there, and what they're doing. This applies even if you move into a new setting in the same scene, like when you go from the car to the garage to the house.

This is a basic skill of fiction. Be sure you're doing it.

There are exceptions to this. Sometimes you *want* your reader confused about the setting, as when you're trying to disguise it from the reader to conceal someone's identity or location. But this is exceedingly rare. Most of the time you want your readers to be able to visualize your story, right? Help them out. Add establishing shots to every scene and every new setting in your book.

chapter 38

THE FULL SENSORY SWEEP

Many beginning novelists fail to describe their new setting (or character) at all. Or they give brief hints, like "outside" or "a spacious room." But when they do think to describe a location, they usually do so by describing what the place *looks like*. A visual description. That's fine. We need to know what the eye can see. But it's not enough. It doesn't give the reader a full sense of what the place is like.

When you go somewhere, what do you notice? Let's say you park your car and get out in the parking lot behind a row of restaurants at dinnertime. Do you mainly notice what you *see*? Not if you're hungry. You'll notice the tantalizing *smells* that are drifting by on the breeze.

If you step outside your house in the middle of a heat wave in Phoenix (or a cold snap in Minneapolis), are you mainly going to notice what the place looks like? Not likely. You'll feel the heat (or the cold) slam into you and punish you for leaving the climate-controlled house.

The sound of a jackhammer or a chickadee. The grit of sand in your teeth at the beach. The feeling of a hot plastic car seat. These are all part of how we sense the world. Therefore they should all be part of how you describe your fictional world. It's how you make your fictional world *believable* to the reader.

Whenever you introduce a new setting, you must describe it for the reader. When you're thinking about how to describe your new setting, go through the five senses to consider which ones might be presenting interesting detail your character could notice.

The subtle sensory detail is very often what *sells* your setting to the reader. Who can forget the story in the Gospel of John in which the aroma of the perfume could be smelled throughout the house? Doesn't that place you in that first-century Jewish home? I once wrote a scene in which a woman opens a hot oven and feels the heat push back her bangs, and it was that sensory detail that made the scene come alive to some readers.

Don't be mechanical about this. Don't give a report from each of the five senses for every setting in your book, no matter how much of a stretch it is. Instead, every time just *consider* what the viewpoint character's senses might realistically be telling him at this moment in this place. Find one or two telling details from the other four senses to augment what can be seen with the eyes.

And don't forget internal senses, like pain, hunger, seasickness, or even feelings of dread, joy, or regret. Certain senses will elicit internal feelings, too. Like what happens to your stomach whenever you smell a dentist's office. …

Add sensory descriptions to virtually every description of your new settings, and you'll help the reader suspend disbelief and enter fully into the world of your story.

chapter 39

COMPARISONS

Neurologists tell us the brain works by using comparisons. It analyzes any input, like what someone says or the appearance of a work of art, and compares it to information it has stored in the past.

"Hmm, the way she said that sounds like how she talked when she was really mad at me last week. I think she may be mad." Or, "Okay, this painting has a color palette that reminds me of warm and comfortable things. I think I like it."

The brain is always trying to find meaning or gain a handle on what's going on. It does this primarily by comparing the current thing to known and stored data.

Your characters in fiction ought to be using comparisons to understand and interpret their lives, too. And certainly your reader needs these similes to gain a handle on what she's looking at in your world. Comparisons and similes communicate wonderfully when you're describing locations (and new characters) in your fiction because we, your readers, thoroughly relate to them in our own lives. It's how we think, too.

Let's say you walk into a football stadium you've never been to. Maybe you're on a cell phone with a friend who couldn't make it. She wants to know what the stadium looks like because her boyfriend will be playing down on the field, and she wants to picture it in her mind.

(Did you notice the implied request for a comparison in what she asked for? She wanted to know what the stadium looked *like*. To what, she was asking, might it be *compared?*)

So you say, "Well, it's kind of like Richland High School's stadium, but the scoreboard is bigger. And it doesn't have the big press box like the Wildcats' stadium, but it does have these concrete tunnels that go under the stands. Do you remember when we saw the playoff game at the college last year? It reminds me a lot of that stadium."

When your viewpoint character enters a new setting, his brain will immediately try to describe it. Giving an establishing shot is very helpful, as is including sensory information, but the final component is a good comparison.

COMPARISONS DO DOUBLE DUTY

The great thing about a comparison is that it not only tells the reader what the place looks or seems like, it also tells you something about the character doing the describing. It sets the scene, *and* it characterizes the viewpoint character.

For instance, when I proposed to my wife I had a ring for her, but I was still waiting for the ring I really wanted her to use as her engagement ring. That one was coming in the mail from my grandmother. When the ring finally arrived, I called my fiancée and tried to describe to her what the ring looked like. I described it in words that were brilliant, evocative, and, above all, romantic.

I said it looked like a silver volcano.

It *did* look like a silver volcano. It had a circular … I don't know … *mound* of white gold that encircled a diamond. Kind of like a flat-topped volcanic mountain with a caldera at the top. I thought it was a great description, and something about the diamond being formed by the geologic pressures of the volcano seemed fitting to me.

Okay, did the comparison communicate? Kind of. Not in the way I'd hoped. Happily, she still married me! But do you see how the comparison did double duty? Not only did it (sort of) describe the ring, it also described me. It showed that when it comes to romantic poetry and a sense of the moment, I pretty much stink.

In your fiction, let your viewpoint characters use comparisons to describe new settings (and characters). "It looked about the size of a basketball court," "She reminded me of a fat version of my aunt Opal," and "It tasted like a combination of Grape-Nuts and cod liver oil."

The more bizarre the location being described, the more the brain reaches for comparisons. This applies especially to those of us who enjoy creating alien worlds and never-before-imagined creatures.

> The thing was enormous, larger than a school bus. Like a squirrel on human growth hormone. A giant, *Honey, I Blew*

> *Up the Marsupial* kind of thing. It jumped around in little hops, like a cricket on a garage floor. And it always seemed disoriented when it landed, as if every impact shook its brain loose for a second.

Now, you can picture that, right? Can you see how helpful the comparisons were? Harness the power of word pictures for your own fiction.

Like these other components of description, you don't have to use a comparison every time. Don't get formulaic about any of these description tools. But use them generously. And I've yet to see a setting description that wasn't helped by a comparison or word picture.

Remember to keep your comparisons consistent with your viewpoint character. If you've brought an alien to twenty-first-century Earth, don't have him compare a room to a disco club. If your viewpoint character is a woman who's never been out of Saudi Arabia, don't let her compare something to Texas Stadium. And if you're in a fantasy world, don't have a character compare a room to a racquetball court.

Put together, the tools of the establishing shot, sensory information, and well-chosen comparisons will help your reader picture the locations you're setting your scenes in. A reader who can picture your locations is an engaged reader, and an engaged reader keeps reading your novel.

chapter 40

DESCRIBE ACTUAL PLACES

A great way to sell the authenticity of a setting is to describe an actual place.

Go to the web and the library and find photos of Scotland or New York City or wherever to draw inspiration for the settings in your novel. Select photos from design magazines to be the rooms of your protagonist's house. Pick at least one photo for each setting in your book.

Better yet, *go* to a place with your journal and just describe it. What do you see, smell, and hear? What does this place remind you of? What are the details that make this place distinct from others like it? How many people are here, and what do they tend to do? Take a few shots with your camera. Video is even better.

When you sit down to write the description for that scene, pull out the photos and simply describe what you see there. Read your journal and copy that stuff down. Watch the video and be reminded of the dominant sounds and the way the light played on the grass. Doing this is much easier, and results in a more authentic description, than making something up in your head.

If all you have to work with is a photo, you may very well need to make up the sounds, smells, temperatures, and tastes of the place, but at least the visual descriptions will be compelling and authentic. And very often you can invent logical sensory information based on what you imagine would be going on in the photo.

A photo will help you with all the procedures in this Description section, actually. Look for the comparisons the photo conjures up in your mind. If you have a wide-enough angle, you actually *have* an establishing shot. You can describe how many people are there, what they're wearing, what the weather was doing, and so on.

IT WORKS ON PEOPLE, TOO

You can use a photo to describe your characters, too. Many novelists "cast" their novels the way filmmakers cast their movies, sometimes using models in Sears catalogs or even movie stars to populate their books. This is fine, so long as you steer clear of identifying the people so precisely that the "any resemblance to actual individuals is purely coincidental" disclaimer becomes a lie.

Using photos of real people can help your character descriptions and even your thinking about what they might be like as characters. People watching at the mall is great for casting your novel, too, but it's harder to remember what people look like when you do it that way (and taking their pictures without having them sign a release can get you in trouble).

Every setting and character in your novel must be described. Using photos of or visits to actual places, buildings, vehicles, and people can give your fiction that ring of authenticity and veracity readers love. It can sell your setting.

chapter 41

USE WORD CHOICE TO SET THE MOOD

In Chapter 35 I talked about what I consider an advanced technique in fiction. That one was about using your viewpoint character's voice as narrator. In this chapter I want to talk about another advanced technique. When you describe your setting, use the opportunity to set the mood you're trying to create.

SAY WHAT?

Here's an example in setting mood through word choice. I'm going to describe the same place three times but set three different moods. The place: a house in the suburbs.

EXAMPLE 1

> A shadow lay over the yard like a grave cloth. The grass was long and unkempt. Against the bole of a withered oak lay a child's ball shrouded by the creeping Bermuda. The features of the house shimmered in the blaze of the afternoon, blurred beyond recognition to the unwary stranger.

Okay, a bit cheesy, maybe, but you get the point. Not a fun place to go.

EXAMPLE 2

> Zinnias blossomed against the cherry tree beside the front porch, their sun-kissed inner circles wreathed in bashful pink. At the base of the grand oak, a mother rabbit led her furry litter out from the shade of a rhododendron's lacy leaves. She sniffed the breeze with delicate nostrils, brushed her eye with a paw, and bounded into the sun.

Ah, a more pleasant place, yes? A Disney moment.

EXAMPLE 3

The dirt showed through the grass in brown scars. The grass that remained was brittle and sharp, like a smoker's eyebrows. Signs remained of the home's luxuriant past—the garden path, the children's toys, the "Home of the Week" sign out front—but they lay wasted. An American flag still fluttered on its pole, but the sun had washed it out to a milky translucence, and its trailing edge was shredded. It hung from only one tether, twisting in the wind like a castaway's last cry for rescue.

Depressed yet?

I was describing the same place in all three passages: A yard, grass, some trees, and stuff on the lawn. But I created vastly different feelings for the scene that could then take place there.

I did this by means of three tricks. First, I selected different details to point out each time. All the things I mentioned could be there in the yard each time—the flag, the bunny, the child's ball—but by plucking out specific details that supported the mood I was after, I was able to construct different images in your mind.

Second, I made heavy use of word pictures and comparisons. You'll notice I never resorted to personification, in which I could've brought inanimate objects to life ("the weeds tried to choke the joy from the yard," that sort of thing). The similes were sufficient.

Third, I chose my vocabulary carefully. In the first one, I used words like *grave cloth, bole, shrouded, withered,* and *creeping.* In the second, I used *blossomed, furry, bashful,* and *bounded.* (Plus a bunny—you can never go wrong with a furry bunny if you want to paint a happy mood.) In the third, I used *wasted, brittle,* and *cry,* plus images of regret and loneliness.

Actually, I did a fourth thing to create the mood I was after. This one's so subtle I didn't realize I was doing it until I stepped back and took a look. I used words that "sounded to the eye" like other words that helped paint the picture I was going for. For instance, I used *shimmered* when I was thinking *shivered.* I used *cherry* to sound close to *cheery.* And I used *lacy* to sound like *lazy,* as in relaxed.

Pretty cool, huh? I've gone a bit overboard to illustrate, but you can achieve the same effect with a less heavy hand simply by being mindful of the mood you're trying to create.

You can do this to convey the narrator's mood, too. Indeed, you could combine both advanced techniques in this book into one. You've got a viewpoint character who is the narrator, and now you want to illustrate his mood, so you do so by having him describe things in ways that reveal his inner state. Now we're really at heady altitude.

The same house and yard might look all three of these ways at different points in the story depending on how the viewpoint character is feeling at the moment. We all see things we want to see—or fear—and your characters are no different.

So try it. Do you have a scene you want your reader to perceive as happy, frightening, or sad? Do you want the reader to arrive at the scene feeling wary, disarmed, or flush with young love? Then take out your paint kit (your thesaurus) and begin selecting your palette.

It should work the other way around, too. If you're about to write a scene that is supposed to be scary, be mindful of the images and vocabulary you use to describe the setting. You should probably remove the happy family of bunnies, in other words.

Your words are setting a mood for your scenes, whether you think about them or not. I'm just asking you to think about them. You want your descriptions to help set the mood you're after, not work against you.

Descriptions are like paintings. An artist will choose her tools carefully. The brushes, the canvas, the paints, the colors, and more. All of these help her convey the image and feeling she wants to create in the painting.

So it is in your fiction. It's the words and images you choose in your description that convey the mood you want to create for your scenes. Be mindful of your tools, and paint away!

chapter 42
BEATS

A beat is a segment of narration that informs the reader what's happening in a scene, gives her a good fix on the setting, shows characters' movements, and helps you manage the perceived passage of time in your story.

The term *beat* comes from play scripts and screenplays, and perhaps from music before that. In scripts, when the playwright wrote "a beat," it meant that he wanted the actor to pause a moment before speaking the next line.

For example:

LOUISE

Tom, don't come in here with that. Unless ...

[a beat]

... unless you mean to bury it.

The playwright wanted the actress to pause there, so he indicated the pause by inserting a beat.

Beats usually go along with a significant revelation in the script or some other moment when the character should either hesitate before speaking or take a moment to absorb the impact of something that has just happened.

A beat means a pause, a moment of silence, in the middle of a dialogue scene.

USING BEATS IN FICTION

There are times in your scenes when you need a character to pause a moment before going on to the next thing. You want to give time for the character to process something, absorb the impact of a statement, or overcome a reluctance. How do you imply that pause? With beats!

Let's say SueAnne has just announced to her boyfriend that she's pregnant. She's dropped the bomb on him, and you want to show him reeling from the impact.

First I'll show the moment without a beat:

> "Bobby Lee, I need you to come here a minute."
>
> "Not now, SueAnne, the boys're waitin'."
>
> "No, sweet thing, I need you to come here right now. I got something I need to tell you."
>
> "What is it?"
>
> "I'm pregnant."
>
> "Are you serious?"
>
> "Yes, I'm serious."
>
> "What are you going to do about it?"
>
> "What do you mean what am I going to do? I'm going to have your baby."
>
> "No, you ain't."
>
> "You can't mean … "
>
> "Durn right."

Did you sense how rushed the scene feels? When she drops the p-bomb on him, he seems to have taken no time to absorb the news. It seems like he's got his reply already on his lips, as if he were expecting her to say this.

Dialogue scenes without beats are like old Frank Capra movies in which the hero and heroine have a rapid-fire banter that comes so quickly it seems they're not listening to one another, that they had their next lines prepared and ready before the other person even spoke. It worked for dear Frank, but it won't work for your story.

Now, you as the author may very well have *imagined* Bobby having this tremendous pause when he hears the news. You may have seen him widen his eyes, do a double take, clutch his heart, and sit down. But none of that is there for the reader to see. As far as the reader sees, he moves without pause or even slowing down to his next line of dialogue.

As they say in theater, "If it ain't on the page, it ain't on the stage."

Here is the scene again with a few rudimentary beats:

> SueAnne tapped the cushion beside her. "Bobby Lee, I need you to come here a minute."

"Not now, SueAnne," Bobby said, settling his cap just right in the mirror. "The boys're waitin'."

"No, sweet thing, I need you to come here right now." She swallowed carefully. "I got something I need to tell you."

"What is it?"

Here it was, her moment. She made her voice as sweet as she could. "I'm pregnant."

The change that came across Bobby's face was so dramatic it would've been funny on any other day. His sneer disappeared, and his face went slack. His eyes widened, and his mouth dropped open. "Are you serious?"

"Yes, I'm serious."

He blinked at her twice. Then he seemed to recover his senses. He stood up straight, and the sneer returned. Once again she was no more than a thing to him. "What are you going to do about it?"

"What do you mean what am I going to do? I'm going to have your baby."

"No, you ain't."

She knew it. Momma had been right. "You can't mean ..."

"Durn right."

See the difference? Okay, maybe I overcompensated and put a few too many beats in there, but I wanted you to be able to feel the difference.

With the beats, you felt the pauses in dialogue. There was a rhythm to the scene the second time through. An ebb and flow. Not so much with the first version.

Let's look at the three main things these beats added to our scene: character actions, tie-downs to the setting, and management of perceived time.

BEATS TELL US CHARACTERS' ACTIONS

In the first version, all we had were the characters' spoken words. They might've been interesting, but it's an incomplete picture. There's no picture at all, actually.

I added those beats to describe what was happening in the scene. From beats we learned that SueAnne was sitting and Bobby was standing. We learned what Bobby's face did when he heard the news. We got more of a *picture* of what was happening in the scene.

What's more, the beats flowed right along with the action of the scene. In fact, the beats actually *created* the flow of the scene.

When you don't include descriptions of what the characters are doing, your reader loses track of what's going on and can find it difficult to understand the nuances of meaning your characters are displaying. It's like the difference between an e-mail and a phone call, and between a phone call and an in-person conversation. The more ability you have to read the other person's tone of voice, body language, and expression, the more likely you are to correctly understand what he's saying. That's what beats do for you in fiction.

BEATS TIE THE READER INTO THE SETTING

In the first version of our scene we had no clue where these two characters were. Were they in a car? Were they inside or outside? Were they alone or in a crowd? Was it day or night? What was the weather like? Where were the characters in relation to one another?

Now, the second version didn't answer all those questions, but it did give you a better feel for where they were. They were in a house, apparently alone (at least in this room), and SueAnne was sitting while Bobby was standing by the mirror. You can picture that, can't you? At least you have a better picture of the "stage" now than you did with the original version.

Without beats that refer to the environment, a conversation becomes nothing but talking heads. It might as well be radio—but at least in radio they use sound effects to clue you in.

Long dialogue sequences, as I've mentioned already, are like helium balloons. They have a tendency to become detached from the world and float away into the heavens, coming finally to reside in some foggy nebula. And that's no fun to read (unless you're writing about foggy nebulae, that is).

Like a hot-air balloon, conversations need tie-downs to the setting, or they will float away. Go through your manuscript looking for long dialogue passages. Then find a place, every fifth line of dialogue or so, to give us a note about how the characters are relating to the environment (standing, eating, changing the radio station, etc.), or your reader will lose track of what's going on.

Again, *you* may be envisioning all these interactions with the setting beautifully in your head. But unless you write them into the manuscript, they will not exist for the reader.

BEATS MANAGE THE PACING OF YOUR SCENE

This third use of beats is the closest to the original, theatrical meaning of the word. But it goes beyond pauses.

In video editing the editor sits in front of a console that has one or more knobs that give him fine control over the playback of the footage being edited. Regular speed, slow speed, fast-forward, fast-rewind, slow rewind, etc., are all at his command. He needs this kind of control to be able to do detailed work.

Beats—their presence or absence, and their length, long or short—are like playback knobs for your story. If you want a moment in your story to go by quickly, you can do that with beats. If you want a massive pause followed by a shocking change, you can do that with beats. Whatever speed you want this particular moment in this particular scene to go, you manage that with beats.

Here's the rule: The longer the text you use to create the beat, the longer the perceived pause. More text in a beat means more time elapsed in silence.

Back in our scene we had some shorter beats earlier on, like SueAnne patting the cushion or taking a deep breath before dropping her news. These would've been hardly perceptible pauses in real life. But when Bobby hears the news, the paragraph beat is much longer; his face changes, his sneer disappears, he reacts. There's more text in this beat, and that simulates a longer pause. A much longer pause. It gives him time to process and react and try to find his words.

Without the pause, it would've seemed like the first version, like he either didn't really hear her or he already knew about it. Either way, it would've seemed like he hadn't taken any time to absorb and process. That is not what you want here.

Do you see what the beats did? They managed the pacing of the scene. I was like a film editor inserting or removing pauses in order to make the scene flow at exactly the rhythm I wanted. That's what beats do for you in fiction. If you include no beat between two lines of dialogue, you imply there was no interval between those lines. If you want to simulate a pause of any kind, insert a beat.

BEATS IN ACTION SCENES

The longer your beat, the slower the moment. A long paragraph slows the eye down and causes it to linger. In a strange physiological way, it calms you down to read a long paragraph. It takes the reader longer to physically get through the thing. This implies a longer pause in story time.

The corollary is also true: The shorter the paragraph, the more brisk that moment feels to the reader. Use this to your advantage when writing action scenes. As you get closer and closer to the climactic moment, use shorter and shorter paragraphs. Long paragraphs are like lazy summer afternoons. Short paragraphs indicate urgency and quickness.

When things get fast and furious in your scene, start breaking things down into shorter and shorter paragraphs. On a subconscious level it will feel to your reader that things are beginning to hurtle downhill. She won't understand why, but she will suddenly feel that things are going fast. She'll be whipping the pages aside and feeling breathless. At the end of the scene she'll feel, well, beat.

This is because the shorter paragraphs make the pages go by faster. The eye moves quickly through small, easily digestible paragraphs and consumes page after page.

Conversely, if you want something to feel leisurely and relaxed (like when you're setting the reader up to be surprised when the alien drool monster bursts through the wall and eats the hero's best friend), give lots of longer paragraphs and longer sentences. (But don't let any paragraph go longer than eight lines.)

Take hold of beats. They are among the most useful and powerful tools you have at your disposal. Use them as a master craftsman, and your reader will arise and call you blessed.

chapter 43
PAYOFF WITHOUT A PLANT

I like to teach novelists not to mix metaphors in their fiction. Few things scream mediocrity as a lame sentence that has galloped through jumbled images like a jigsaw puzzle on thin ice.

And yet I'm going to start by using a mixed metaphor: plant and payoff.

What I'm getting at with these terms is regarding this principle in fiction: You must establish that something exists before you can use it—and if you establish something exists, you must use it.

Let's say on page 350 of your novel you need your protagonist to jump into a helicopter and fly away from the bad guys. But have you previously established he knows how to fly helicopters? You better have.

Somewhere earlier in your story it needs to come out—preferably by you *showing* him flying around in similar craft—that he knows how to pilot such things. Then when he does it in a crucial moment, it's already been established (planted) in the reader's mind he can do this. If you want to have the *payoff* (he can fly helicopters), you'd better have previously included the plant.

There's a corollary to this: If you plant that he can fly helicopters, that had better be important for us to know later in the story.

A-PLANTING WE WILL GO

The *plant* is when you let the reader know something exists, that something is important, or that a character has an ability or piece of knowledge. The *payoff* is when you use that thing you've planted.

In the original *Star Wars* movie, we think Luke Skywalker is toast in the Death Star trench because his wingmen have been taken away, and Darth Vader is moving in for the kill. As far as we know, he's completely unprotected. But then in swoops Han Solo in the *Millennium Falcon* to save the day.

"Oh, yeah!" we say. "Han didn't come with them. He would've been unaccounted for. That totally works! Go, Luke, go!"

The plant was that we knew in the back of our minds that Han Solo was in the area but not with the attack group. The payoff was him arriving just in time.

At the climax of *The Lord of the Rings*, Frodo comes to the Cracks of Doom to throw the ring into the lava, but he stops. He's failing at the last moment. He's going to give in to the ring and go do bad things. But then out of nowhere Gollum pounces and wrestles with Frodo for the ring, ultimately saving him from his own bad choices.

Though Gollum had been out of our thoughts for a while, we did know he was still unaccounted for. He was out there, on the loose. That was the plant, though the reader wasn't aware it had been planted. When Gollum arrives, just at the crucial moment (the payoff), it makes complete sense to us.

These examples work because both plant and payoff were present.

But what if there had been no plant, and yet the payoff was still there?

What if we had never known of any character named Han Solo, and then at the climactic moment of the movie this complete stranger zooms up and blasts Darth Vader? We'd be like, "Huh? Who's that guy? What's going on? That totally doesn't work."

What if we'd never heard of Gollum? And then, right when the story needed someone to come in and save Frodo from his bad choices, this odd creature jumps up and takes the ring? We'd be like, "Um, what was that weird thing? What a stupid ending!"

Those would be examples of *payoff without plant.*

Because the important element hadn't been established earlier (i.e., planted), it feels external to the story. It feels like an intrusion of something that didn't belong, not something that arose organically from the story.

But go back and find a place to introduce those characters earlier, and suddenly it all feels right.

GOT FERTILIZER?

It sounds silly and obvious, but I see payoff without plant all the time in aspiring novelists' fiction.

People the audience hadn't met before become the key group to rescue the hero at the end of the story. Treasures we hadn't even heard about before become the thing the hero acts like he's been after all along. Characters we hadn't met die, and the protagonist is all broken up about it, but we're like, "Who's that?"

That's what a payoff without a plant is. If you don't introduce important things early on, we don't believe or care about them when you bring them out later. A protagonist who for three hundred pages has been a pipe fitter and then in the climax suddenly knows how to defuse a thermonuclear device is going to feel *wrong* to the reader. A car that for the whole story has been on death's door but then in the climax becomes a world-caliber race car is going to strike the reader as being completely unbelievable.

And it all would've been solved if only the crucial aspect of that person or thing had been established somewhere earlier in the book.

If you have characters whose special abilities are going to be called upon in the climax, you'd better be very sure you've revealed these abilities loud and clear to the reader before then. If the key to the whole novel is the switch the hero has to flip to avert the earth-dissolving disaster, you'd better be double sure you've talked about the switch earlier in the book.

PAYOFF WITHOUT PLANT IN DESCRIPTION

If you're going to have a person or part of the setting be important in the scene, you must establish that he or it is there when you give your initial description of the setting. If you don't, and then you suddenly refer to the person or thing halfway through your scene, it will seem as if he or it has just appeared there in a cloud of pixie dust.

For instance, let's say there's a scene in a cavern. The initial description establishes for us there are three people here, the cavern is dark and dank, and the only light comes from three torches set in sconces on the walls. The scene progresses for several pages. Then suddenly the hero walks over to the chasm and drops the sword into the abyss.

You'd say, "Huh? What sword? And *what chasm?*" Because the author hadn't planted that there was an abyss here and that the character was wearing his sword, those things seem to appear magically just as they're needed in the scene.

Chances are, that's how it went when the author was writing it. She got to that part of the scene and went, "Ooh, there should totally be a bottomless pit here, and he should drop something into it, like a sword." So she writes that. The trouble is she didn't go back to the earlier part of the scene and write in a mention of these items.

And that's all she needed to do. She just needed to scroll back up to the setting description and put in a sentence about the dangerous chasm from which noxious fumes arose in gusts. Then she'd need to find a subtle way early on to have her hero adjust his sword on his belt. Just a simple mention of the thing is enough to plant it for the reader.

Magically appearing items and people that conveniently manifest for the first time deep into a scene are things that frustrate and disorient your reader. A payoff with no plant will just anger your reader. And nobody wants that.

chapter 44

PLANT WITHOUT PAYOFF

If you plant something but then don't use it, it's a plant without payoff. To the reader, it feels like a red herring, and it's equally frustrating. Worse, it makes you look like you don't know what you're doing as a novelist.

THE BIG PAYOFF

Imagine you're reading a story, and the author goes to great lengths to set up that the protagonist is a whiz with numeric patterns. There are pages and pages of how good she is with these. We're thinking *A Beautiful Mind* kind of thing.

As we're going along in the story, we're waiting for that information to be important. We've assumed that you're showing us this because it's going to come into play later. So we're set up for it. We're ready. As situations develop in the story we're like, "Okay, I'll bet she sees some pattern in the flower arrangement and solves the mystery!" We're totally engaged.

But the rest of the story goes by, and the protagonist never uses this pattern recognition. Not once. Has this pleased the reader? Not a chance.

The reader feels ripped off and angry. "Wait a minute, here. You made me remember all that about the numeric patterns, and you never *used* it? It was never important? Why did I waste the time to retain that in ready memory then? The whole reason I got interested in your story is because I thought you were going to use that."

Plant and payoff are like bookends. If you have either one but don't have its matching opposite on the other side, all the books fall off onto the floor. Figuratively speaking.

Make sure you don't spend page space talking about something you're not going to use. Don't mention something about a character that you don't come back to later. And if you *do* spend page space establishing something, you'd better use it.

Better yet, if you're not going to use it, don't talk about it. We assume that what you talk about, what you make us pay attention to, will be important later. Don't violate that expectation.

I love the movie *Night at the Museum*. It's a hysterical film. But it has a plant without a payoff. It's small, but it still irritates me.

Rebecca tells Larry that all the time the historical Sacagawea was leading Lewis and Clark's expedition she was carrying her baby on her back. But Sacagawea in the museum has no baby. So right away we're looking for the baby. Is it lost? Then we see Teddy Roosevelt searching for something in relation to Sacagawea. And Sacagawea herself is looking kind of forlorn and distracted, as if she's looking for her baby. We're completely set up for the epic search for Sacagawea's baby.

But it never happens. We're thinking there's a baby in peril somewhere, but it's never spoken of again.

That's plant without payoff. We thought it was a major plot point, but it ended up being just a little factoid the writer threw in because he'd researched it. It angered viewers (well, one viewer, anyway) because he thought it was going to be important, but it ended up not being so. Anyway, where *is* her baby?

PLANT AND PAYOFF IN BALANCE

Plant and payoff have to be in correct proportion to one another. If you spend several pages and scenes setting something up, it had better be very important later. And if something *is* very important later, it had better have been set up with a sufficiently long plant scene earlier and not just mentioned in passing.

In Tom Clancy's massive novel *The Sum of All Fears*, he spends probably one hundred pages on a storyline about giant redwood tree trunks that have been felled in the Pacific Northwest and are being shipped to Japan, where they will be used in a temple. While at sea a fierce storm breaks out, and the logs are dropped into the ocean.

For at least one hundred pages you've been reading about these trees. You've learned about where they grew, how they were felled, how they were loaded onto a ship, and the difficulties the ship has as it passes through a storm. The logs might even come loose. Because you've been reading so much about these logs, you're convinced that they are very important to the story. What kind of payoff could it be, you wonder.

Then, deep into the novel, a submarine surfaces in the storm to receive a message on its antenna. But, oh no, something hits the antenna, and now it doesn't work.

That was it. One hundred pages of following these stupid tree trunks, and the only thing the entire storyline was there for was to have something bonk a silly antenna! Why had the author wasted so much of my time on those logs? The payoff was definitely not in proportion to the plant. He could've spent one paragraph introducing a big sea turtle and had *that* bonk the infernal antenna.

Make sure you have planted everything you want to be important later, and make sure you give a payoff to everything you plant. And keep them in proportion.

But whatever you do, don't mix your metaphors!

Focus on the Craft: DIALOGUE

The final "Focus on the Craft" section in *The Art & Craft of Writing Christian Fiction* has to do with dialogue.

So we've had these sections on character, showing versus telling, point of view, description, and now dialogue. I think that's fitting because those are what I believe to be the most important areas of craftsmanship for the novelist. Get those things right, my friend, and you will almost certainly become a published author.

Dialogue seems so simple. Just have people talk, for crying out loud. What's so hard about that? And yet the only thing that's simple about dialogue is how easy it is to do badly.

In this section of chapters I'm going to cover four secrets of good dialogue, and I'm going to examine how to handle profanity in Christian fiction.

And I'll start it off with probably the most common remark I make to beginning novelists: When it comes to dialogue, stick with *said*.

chapter 45

STICK WITH *SAID*

I'm not exactly sure why novelists deviate from having characters simply *say* things: "Interesting," he said.

Why do they feel that *said* wouldn't work? To avoid using *said* they insist their characters not say words but growl, proclaim, or laugh them out, as if such a thing were possible. Try moaning out words. You're either moaning or you're speaking. Not both.

Maybe it's because these novelists feel they've used *said* too many times already, and they want to spruce up their prose. Writing teachers recommend authors avoid repetition, so maybe that's why writers jettison *said* (and *asked*) and crack open their thesauri.

Anything but *said* is painfully visible. It stands out and says, "Hey, look at me: I used a clever word that was not *said!*" As an author, though, you may decide you don't want to be visible, remember? You may want to be invisible.

Terms besides *said* are usually either redundant ("Watch out!" she warned), physically impossible ("Hello," he breathed), or both ("I can't breathe!" she gasped).

Now, if you're going to have someone shout, whisper, or mutter, I suppose you're okay. Because you really can shout, whisper, and mutter out your words. But you can't chortle, guffaw, or sigh them out. Nor can you (or should you) opine, comment, venture, offer, counter, or bluster out your words.

Here's the rule: If you can't actually make intelligible utterances with the verb you're using instead of *said*, then, well, *stick to said.*

Can you really snarl out, "I love you, my dear"? Try it.

Asked is okay, too. You don't need to say, "What is it?" she questioned. Or "Is that the best you can do?" she queried.

Another reason authors may use words besides *said* is they want to avoid using modifiers. Rather than write, "Never!" she said fiercely, they'd rather write, "Never!" she barked. But I'm telling you this looks silly.

It's really okay to use *said* and then tell how something was said ("He's back!" she said breathlessly). That's a much better solution than using some other word that is so odd it kicks the reader right out of your story.

Said is invisible, and invisibility is what you're striving for. Other words stick out like flares at midnight, eliminating the stealth quotient you're going for. So avoid them.

Say it with me: "I promise I will stick with *said*!"

chapter 46

GREAT DIALOGUE IS REALISTIC

What makes good dialogue in fiction? Is it snappy one-liners or trendy phrases? Is it innuendo or inflection or devastating irony? Perhaps it's the unforgettable line: "The problems of three little people don't amount to a hill of beans in this crazy world."

Maybe it's truth that makes dialogue great. Digging down to the essence of the human condition. "I am not an animal! I am a human being! I … am … a man!"

Dialogue in movies gives us some of our favorite moments: "Frankly, my dear …" or "I've got a bad feeling about this" or "The horror … the horror."

Every novelist wants her lines of dialogue to be as powerful and memorable as these. But how? What's the secret?

And you need to find out because there are acquisitions editors out there (the ones who love fiction, primarily) who will skip over everything in your proposal and flip straight to a section of dialogue in your sample chapters. If you've done your dialogue poorly, they'll put the proposal away right then and won't look at anything else.

I submit to you that I wasn't far off when I suggested it might be truth that creates good dialogue. I believe dialogue is great when it is *authentic*. Dialogue must be realistic, layered, and right for the character and the moment.

GET REAL

Realism is probably the hardest thing to capture in fiction dialogue. How can you create dialogue that sounds like it might actually be spoken?

You can't just type up transcripts of actual conversations. Have you ever really paid attention to how we talk? Imagine Brock and Cammie having this conversation:

> "Did you get the ...?"
>
> "Nah. I thought we'd, uh, take the ... thing."
>
> "Okay. Move the shoes, please. So I guess you, you know, are okay with ...?"
>
> "Those aren't my shoes. Oh, I saw Francie at the club. She said we wouldn't ... It's like, she doesn't even ..."
>
> "You're kidding. But she's, you know. And besides, why don't you ... I mean, is it too much to ask to ..."

That's all pretty realistic. But it's not exactly easy to read. It's scattered, multithreaded, and incomplete. This is because real conversations are conveyed through tone and body language as much as actual words.

What you're after in fiction dialogue is something that *simulates* reality but is more intelligible than actual speech.

Let's look at the components of realistic-seeming dialogue.

A REAL BOY

First, realistic dialogue is not formal or polite.

> "I believe we will be late if we take that route."
>
> "No, we will not be late. We'll be able to cross over at the Winston Changeover and miss the construction at Seventh."
>
> "Yes, that will be fine."

People don't talk like that. See how nice they are? And see how they take turns and let each other finish complete sentences? Dialogue in real life is much messier (though we need to also keep it intelligible for readers).

> "Don't take Main! You'll make us late. There's—"
>
> "Would you let me drive? We'll take Winston and miss the construction at—"
>
> "Whatever. Just go."

So, lesson one: Don't let dialogue be formal or polite. Don't let your characters take turns and allow one another to express their complete thoughts before speaking.

Second, realistic dialogue is not "on the nose."

Here's an example of on-the-nose dialogue.

> "Bubba, you have bad breath."

"No, Cletus, I do not have bad breath. I brushed my teeth this morning."

"If you had brushed your teeth this morning, you wouldn't have bad breath. That's what Louanne said, anyway."

"Louanne did not say that. She said ..."

By "on the nose" I mean the characters are saying exactly what they mean and responding to exactly what each other actually says. Real-world conversations are not like that.

Words, the deconstructionists tell us, are pitiful vehicles for conveying meaning. And all of us know conversations aren't so much about what is said as what is *meant*.

"Bubba, you have bad breath."

"Dude, look, I'm sorry I dumped your sister. Deal with it."

"She deserves better than that. Better than you."

"Whatever, Cletus. Besides, I brushed this morning."

In real life, and in simulations of real dialogue, we're never really talking sentence to sentence. It's not the words we use so much as the messages imperfectly carried in those words. We're actually talking meaning to meaning, subtext to subtext.

This is why misunderstandings happen so often in e-mails. When you're left with only the words themselves and don't have the benefit of the tone of voice, body language, and inflection that carry 50 percent of the meaning, we don't communicate accurately.

Lesson two: Let your characters communicate with and respond to the subtext beneath their words, not the words themselves. Don't let dialogue be on the nose.

Great fiction dialogue feels realistic. If your book has dialogue that seems real, your book will be set above many unpublished manuscripts out there. If an editor flips straight to a section of dialogue in your proposal, she will begin to believe you might be ready to be published.

chapter 47

GREAT DIALOGUE IS LAYERED

Authentic dialogue is realistic, layered, and right for the character and the moment. Now let's talk about how to make dialogue layered.

What do I mean when I say that dialogue must be *layered*? This mainly goes back to the idea in the previous chapter that conversations don't really take place in a word-to-word manner. It's not the words of the spoken sentences so much as it is the unspoken meaning beneath those words.

For instance, if you're late for work one day, and the boss says, "Nice of you to join us," she's not really meaning what she says. If a non-English speaker heard or read those words, he might think the boss is being polite. But you and I know the boss really meant, "You're late again, and it's disrespectful. Knock it off or suffer the consequences."

Meaning to meaning, not sentence to sentence.

A SEVEN-LAYER CAKE

When we talk to people, we're communicating via subtext. The meaning is *layered* beneath the actual words.

And one of those layers often contains old topics or disagreements the characters haven't resolved. Jibes, digs, and stabs. Private jokes. Covert warnings. Ongoing debates.

For instance: John and Mary are out for dinner with Mark and Martha. All the way to the restaurant, John and Mary have been arguing about whether they should send their rebellious teenage son to boarding school. Now they're in a booth at Chili's talking with their friends.

> "So, Mark," Mary says, "how's your daughter doing? Still an *A* student?"

> "Well, she does all right. She did get a *B* on—"
>
> "I was just wondering because I know she did a year at … what was the name of that boarding school?"
>
> John rolls his eyes. Here we go.
>
> "No, that wasn't actually a boarding school," Martha says. "Bentley is a—"
>
> "And hadn't she been kind of getting in trouble before you sent her there?" Mary asks. "I seem to recall an incident with a boyfriend."
>
> "Mary," John says, "leave it alone."
>
> Martha sits up straighter. "Just what are you implying, Mary?"
>
> "She's not …" John says. "Mary, let it rest."
>
> "What? I'm just saying that their daughter was rebellious before they sent her to a boarding school, and afterward she became an *A* student. Sometimes a boarding school is just what a teenager needs to shape up. That's all I'm saying."
>
> "Fine, you win. We'll send him. Are you happy now?"
>
> The four of them sit in silence. Mary reaches for her strawberry lemonade, and the glass shakes as she lifts it to her lips.

Now, not every dialogue will have these undercurrents of subtext. But you should be on the alert for chances to show it, because many conversations in your book will contain these layers.

We're always carrying an agenda. We're always trying to sneak in a few points or secretly strengthen our case. Conversations are just one more arena in the battle between personalities. It's that way for your characters, too.

chapter 48
GREAT DIALOGUE IS RIGHT FOR THE CHARACTER AND THE MOMENT

If you're watching a movie, how do you know when one character stops talking and another character starts talking? You start hearing a new voice, and you probably see the new character on the screen.

But how do you do it in fiction? How do you distinguish between one character and another? How can the reader tell when one person has stopped speaking and another speaker has started?

I'm not talking about the formatting mechanics in a manuscript that signal when speakers change—though you must master this. Nor am I talking about speech attributions, though those are vital.

GREAT DIALOGUE IS RIGHT FOR THE CHARACTER

If you had three characters speaking together, and you removed all beats and speech attributions—which you shouldn't do, by the way, but bear with me—the reader still ought to be able to know which character is speaking at any time.

How? By the way each character talks, of course. By how he speaks, by what he thinks about that comes out in his words, by the vocabulary he chooses, by his syntax and grammar, and by the length of his sentences.

Great dialogue is dialogue that is right for the character. Just as Jesus was the Word, and everything He said was an expression of who He was at His core, so should it be with your characters.

By their spoken words alone your characters should distinguish themselves to the reader every time they open their mouths. In a sense, the speech they use is all the speech attribution they should need.

In some cases, of course, you need speech attributions, especially when the character is saying something that could be from any character in the scene: "Watch out!" for instance. But for the rest it ought to be clear simply by the way the person speaks.

Here are some classic lines from movies. Can you name who said them?

> "We thought you was a toad!"
>
> "Mmm, help you, I can."
>
> "It's not the years, honey; it's the mileage."
>
> "The pity of Bilbo may rule the fate of many."
>
> "For it is the doom of men that they forget."
>
> "Lawsy, we got to have a doctor. I don't know nothin' 'bout birthin' babies!"
>
> "Of all the gin joints in all the world, she walks into mine."

Answers: (1) Delmar in *O Brother, Where Art Thou?*; (2) Yoda; (3) Indiana Jones; (4) Gandalf; (5) Merlin in *Excalibur*; (6) Prissy in *Gone with the Wind*; (7) Rick in *Casablanca*.

Ah, good memories, eh? Each one of these can take you not only right into the world of the movie it's from but right into the head of the character who said it.

A major component of developing a character is finding his voice, the unique way of speaking that distinguishes him from everyone else in the novel.

I often see unpublished manuscripts (and some published ones) in which all the characters sound the same. And in fiction, if they all sound the same, they all *seem* the same to the reader. Which means you've got a novel of nothing but the same character talking to himself throughout the book. It feels more like the author doing a puppet show and playing all the parts himself than an eyewitness account of what actually happened when real individuals got together for the story.

It also usually results in uneducated people talking exactly like university professors and non-English speakers from Guam sounding exactly like Professor Higgins in London.

Please, for the sake of your story, do the work to be sure each character's dialogue is right for that character.

GOOD DIALOGUE IS RIGHT FOR THE MOMENT

No matter what your particular character sounds like, he or she won't sound the same in every situation. If he has to scream above the noise of a battle, he's not going to speak in full sentences. If she's out of breath from running, she's going to use shorthand.

And yet I see the opposite in some of the manuscripts I work with. No matter what's going on, the characters talk as if it's a calm moment in the drawing room. Don't do that. Make sure the dialogue that comes out of a character's mouth is not only right for him to say, but is right for the context in which he is currently saying it.

Characters also change their vocabulary and other elements of their speech when in different company. His vocabulary may go up when he's speaking with a college professor, or down when he's speaking with a child or non-English speaker. Her volume may go up when speaking with someone hard of hearing, and down when she's in a theater. Be mindful of the context a character is in so her dialogue is correctly suited for that situation.

Characters also change their dialogue based on how they want to be perceived by the person they're speaking with. If she wants to get in good with the boys, a character may suddenly talk about football and refrain from using long words, peppering her remarks with "stuff" and "thing" instead. If he wants to get in good with a girl, a character may drop all the foul language and instead quote scripture or Shakespeare.

If it's the last minute before the bomb goes off, he's not going to be speaking in complete sentences. If she's in an interview, she's not going to use slang. And if she's a young teen texting with her best friend, she's going to text like a teen.

Read over your dialogue and be sure to make it appropriate not only for the moment but for the character saying it.

chapter 49

DIALOGUE REMINDERS

In the previous chapters in this section we've looked at the key components in crafting good dialogue. In this one I survey a number of reminders and quick ideas for making that dialogue as sharp as it can be.

DON'T LET CHARACTERS SAY THINGS TO ONE ANOTHER THAT THEY BOTH ALREADY KNOW

Novelists have characters engage in (or overhear) conversations containing key information as a way of telling the reader backstory.

> "Wow, Frank, that dam built in 1972 by the president of Kazakhstan is sure pretty."
>
> "Why, yes, Jim, it is. I'll bet the president had no idea that it would one day be used in a global politico-social operation in which covert operatives from the United States would penetrate our defenses and topple our government using highly placed traitors loyal to America."
>
> "No, Jim, I'll bet he didn't. Come, you must sit down and rest the knee you injured in 1985 as you were fighting with the mujahideen in Afghanistan."
>
> "Why, thank you, Jim. You are kind."

If you need characters to say things so the reader can learn them, but you don't want to resort to outright telling, the "dumb-puppet trick" is for you.

DON'T USE TELLING IN QUOTATION MARKS

This is closely related to the previous item, but it bears individualized treatment because it's not always in a discussion in which both characters know the details. In this, authors simply have a character let rip with a concise narration of the events of the story.

> "You see, Winifred, John was not always a bad boy. Once he sang in the church choir and swept up after service. But then the dark times came, and John was forced to beg in the streets, which turned his innocence to cynicism and ..."

The only difference between this and simply including a paragraph of backstory is the use of quotation marks. My friend, don't do that. Avoid telling in all its forms.

Once again, the dumb puppet can save the day.

READ YOUR DIALOGUE ALOUD

So much of the stilted, inappropriate, overly polite, and formal dialogue I see would be eliminated if the novelist had simply read her dialogue out loud once. Better yet, get a couple of friends together and hand out scripts. Coach your friends on the personality and attitude of each character and do a little skit.

You will be amazed at how awful and clunky some bits of your dialogue sound when you hear someone actually say them. You will instantly see it when the dialogue is wrong for the moment or the character. You'll probably even find yourself editing it to sound better *as* you read it aloud.

Those are the edits you need to sit down and change right then. However you thought it should be said out loud is how you should change it to read in your manuscript.

The problem is that you've been sitting alone at your computer writing this stuff, free from all intrusions of reality, so the dialogue probably seemed okay. But heard out loud, the defects are immediately evident. Use this technique a few times and you'll begin learning how to write it more naturally the first time.

This is a simple, fun, but seldom used device (and party game!) for finding the right form for your lines of dialogue.

USE SPEECH ATTRIBUTIONS CORRECTLY

By this I mean you shouldn't use more speech attributions than you have to. In general, you should try to cut down on the number of he-saids/she-saids in your dialogue. If it's obvious who is saying it, leave out the speaker attribution. However, if you have more than two characters in the conversation, or if it's simply not obvious who is speaking, you need to use *more* attributions.

The goal is to give exactly the number of attributions you need to keep the reader oriented about who is speaking. If readers are getting confused about it, you need more. If there are only two people in the conversation, and you've drawn their characters so well that their lines of dialogue *are* their speaker attributions, you can cut out quite a few.

And for the love of all that is beautiful and true, stick to *said* in your attributions.

USE BEATS IN YOUR DIALOGUE

You should be using beats for two main purposes in dialogue: tying your reader down to your setting and managing the pacing and rhythm of your scene.

You can also *use beats in place of speech attributions* to help you cut down on the he-saids. Consider this example:

> "Wait, Damien. You need ... " Lucinda pursed her lips. Could she do it? "You need ... to take your umbrella. It might rain." Coward.

In that sentence, there was no "Lucinda said," yet you knew it was Lucinda speaking. The beat served as the speaker attribution. You can use this, too.

CHANGING GEARS

Great dialogue, as we have seen, is authentic. You create authentic dialogue by making it realistic, layered, and right for the character and the moment. Get those things straight, and your dialogue will be memorable and effective.

When it's all said and done, great dialogue does, after all, amount to a hill of beans in this crazy world.

chapter 50

PROFANITY—THE DEBATE

"Frankly, my dear, I don't give a care."

Doesn't quite work, does it? Give a rip? A flip? Frankly, my dear, I don't care one way or the other?

And yet in Christian fiction, profanity is verboten. The prim church ladies who enjoy inspirational fiction want to do so without having to expose themselves to foul language. So how do we portray characters who use profanity if we're not allowed to use it in our books?

Ah, one of the great dilemmas of writing Christian fiction.

Let me hasten to say I actually agree with the prim church ladies. Having to read profanity in something I'm voluntarily reading, and for fun at that, kind of spoils the experience for me. Many people come to Christian fiction to experience good stories but to remain untouched by the vilest elements of the culture.

In my years in Christian publishing I have had a number of disagreements with fellow publishing professionals on this topic. Some feel—quite vehemently—that avoiding profanity is inherently dishonest, inauthentic. The way to reach the lost, they argue, is to show lost people doing lost things and talking the way lost people do and then to show Christians living out their faith in the story.

I acknowledge that this is a valid argument. However, I continue to disagree with the opinion that CBA fiction ought to be laced with profanity. The audience CBA houses (mainstream Christian publishers in North America) reach, after all, is not the lost, no matter how they wish it were so. They don't reach the motorcycle gangs. They reach prim church ladies: white, Protestant soccer moms; Beth Moore group leaders; and precious grandmothers who work in the church nursery. And this audience doesn't want to read "that kind of trash."

Other folks I've talked to in this debate want to include a watered-down version of profanity in Christian fiction. They want the PG-rated vocabulary. The words they prefer usually have a one-to-one correlation with actual profanity.

Still other folks want to eliminate cussing in Christian fiction entirely. I'm of that school of thought.

However, that doesn't help us with our dilemma. How do you create profane characters without resorting to profanity? Or should you darn the torpedoes and use whatever profanity that character would use?

SURVEYING THE SITUATION

Before I wrote this chapter I surveyed some of my published Christian novelist friends to hear how they deal with this issue. Their solutions fell into six major categories.

PROPOSED SOLUTION 1: USE ALL THE PROFANITY YOU WANT

You can always just let your foul characters talk the way they would really talk. Though it pains you (or not) to do so, you can simply let it all hang out and hope your publisher will be open-minded enough to let it stay in the finished manuscript.

One problem with this is your typical CBA publisher will never let you get away with this. And it's not because they're prudes.

See, all it takes to doom your book is one complaint from a little old lady from Pasadena. She marches to the Christian bookstore where she bought the book, complains to the manager, and says she'll never buy from that store again. Quick as that, your book is pulled from the shelves and sent back to the publisher in bulk, along with a nasty letter about how the bookstore owner will never trust that publishing company again.

A variation on this solution is to write your *rough draft* with all the profanity you think should be in there, and then come back through later and use one of the following solutions to replace it.

PROPOSED SOLUTION 2: USE WATERED-DOWN PROFANITY

In this solution you come as close to the real four-letter words as you can, but you use alternate four-letter words that aren't perceived as being as bad as the originals. In other words, you let your characters be as foul-mouthed as you can possibly get away with, while always pushing the envelope.

I'm a big believer in Ephesians 4:29, which says we should allow no unwholesome word to proceed from our mouths, but only those words that work to build up or educate the hearer. So I don't cuss. However, I think the latter phrase in that verse will allow me to tell you what I mean here, for purposes of education.

In this proposed solution, you use words like *crap, dang, heck,* and *geez,* all of which offend me personally but are in the daily vocabulary of many people who love the Lord with all their hearts, so I won't judge.

To me, this solution makes your characters seem like B-level foul mouths. They'd like to really cuss, but their moms won't let them. It's hard to make someone seem really depraved when they always exercise self-control over their tongues and hold back from actual profanity.

In that sense, I think this solution actually works against what you're trying to do: You want to create someone truly foul, but you end up creating a wimp.

PROPOSED SOLUTION 3: WRITE FOR SECULAR PUBLISHERS (OR SELF-PUBLISH)

If you're so committed to authenticity in your art that you can't bear to write something besides what your foul characters would really say, then consider writing for a publisher that doesn't care about bad language.

Namely, a secular publisher. Sometimes you're not writing what these publishers want *unless* you've got profanity throughout your story. You could also make the argument that writing for a secular publisher is how you can reach the lost with your fiction anyway, so maybe that's the path for you.

Self-publishing is another potential outlet for your profanity-laced fiction. Some Christian subsidy publishing houses (like Xulon or Creation House Press) would want to tone down the profanity in your book, but secular self-publishing companies don't care one way or another. So long as you don't say anything in your book that might get them into legal trouble, they're probably okay with whatever comes out of your characters' mouths.

PROPOSED SOLUTION 4: AVOID WRITING PROFANE CHARACTERS

When I asked this question of one of my friends who is a fellow Christian novelist, she had a sort of epiphany. She realized because of this prohibition against profanity in Christian novels, she'd simply avoided writing truly foul characters in her fiction. Such characters had been on the fringe of her stories, but she'd never written one into the middle of her story—which would've obligated her to face this dilemma.

You can do this, too. It's probably the most elegant solution: You don't have to decide whether to let your profane characters use profanity because you simply haven't written any profane characters. Problem solved.

However, someone could make the case that avoiding a major category of person in your stories puts a certain limit on your fiction and your storytelling. That might not be a bad thing. We all limit our story choices anyway, like choosing not to write romance, horror, or YA, so maybe this is the right solution for you.

PROPOSED SOLUTION 5: USE EUPHEMISMS

This is the most commonly employed solution to our dilemma in Christian fiction. In this solution, you let characters be as foul-mouthed as you want them to be—you simply don't spell it out.

> When Jerry learned of Mary's affair, he let us all know exactly how he felt about her character, her physical attributes, and choice aspects of her ancestry.
>
> Louise's anger grew throughout the day. Finally, after kicking her toe on a table leg, she let loose with a string of profanity that left the ochre paint two shades paler.

This kind of thing is the literary equivalent to how old movies used to handle sex scenes. The door shut and the screen faded to black. We knew what was going on, but it wasn't demonstrated for us onstage. You can accomplish the same thing in your fiction.

Incidentally, this *is* the way old novels handled profanity. Here's an example from *A Touch of Death*, a 1953 novel by Charles Williams:

> She didn't like me. And you could see the chords in her throat while she was telling me about it. "Shut up," I said.

In Internet parlance, we speak of *metadata*. That refers to data about data. Metaknowledge is knowledge about knowledge. It's a way of describing something by taking one step back from the thing to tell us what it is and what attributes it has.

This solution to profanity could be called metaprofanity. It's information *about* the profanity. We don't see the swearing itself, but we see a description of the swearing.

You have to be more creative (and use more humor) to write this way. Anybody can write in a cuss word, but it takes real talent to give us the feeling of the cussing without literally spelling it out.

This is probably the solution you should use most of the time.

PROPOSED SOLUTION 6: INVENT A LANGUAGE

You can't do this in most books, obviously. But when you write speculative fiction you have the opportunity to create a whole new language. Characters can swear a blue streak, but because it's a made-up language, no one can possibly be offended.

The cancelled science fiction TV series *Firefly* sort of did this. The solution there was to use bits of Mandarin Chinese when the characters went off into cussing because in the far future the last great superpowers, the U.S. and China, merged, resulting in a merging of their languages.

It's quite convenient to have a swearing language at your disposal. You might be able to do this, too.

Firefly also uses made-up words not derived from Chinese. Characters say "gorram," which is obviously a euphemism for something else, but it's not actually cussing and therefore no one has grounds to be upset. *Battlestar Galactica* used "frak," which again they get away with because it's technically not a word, though it was clear from usage what it meant.

I'm inventing a language for my own epic fantasy. It's mostly English, but I use synonyms for all kinds of things: A gnat is a neener, a squirrel is a scratch, and "okay" is "ulda."

I'm allowing certain characters in my book to cuss like construction workers—but only in this nonsense language. Snoog. Rhyne. Stelnate. Are you offended? Exactly. It allows characters to be profane in their language but not offend readers in our language.

There is a theory that any culture's swearing vocabulary arises from areas in which that culture feels repressed. For instance, French Canadians use parts of a cathedral as their curse words: Oh, tabernacle! Holy sancrist! Apparently they felt oppressed by the church.

If you're making up a culture, why not use this theory to also make up a curse vocabulary that involves whatever they're feeling repressed by (or did feel repressed by back in the day, when such things were being invented)?

In my fantasy novel, my characters feel overly oppressed by high taxation. "Well, I'll be taxed," is a common epithet in their tongue.

Such a solution allows you to be as crass as you want, using words or terms that are, in and of themselves, inoffensive.

A BETTER WAY

Those are the main solutions for showing profane characters in Christian fiction. Hopefully, one is for you.

But now let me tell you what I think is the real issue and challenge for you.

chapter 51
PROFANITY—THE SOLUTION

We've looked at six proposed solutions for how Christian novelists can handle profanity in their fiction. Now let's look at a better way.

Because I value show over tell, let me illustrate.

DWAYNE

Little blond Barbie dolls. Cute.

Dwayne moved through the house with the silence of a roach. He entered the girl's playroom and crept inside. Must be nice to have a playroom *and* a big room of your own. He bent over the large dollhouse, where a blond plastic bimbo sat askew in her chair having a burger and fries with a red-headed plastic bimbo.

Moonlight cast soft shadows on the toy cabinets and dress-up bin and pink beanbag chairs in the playroom. Typical. Delicious.

Dwayne picked up the blond doll and caressed its molded smile with the tip of his hunting knife. The stiff yellow hair fell across the edge of the blade.

Hmm.

He snatched the locks in his thumb and fingers, slightly less dexterous because of the rubber gloves. He put his left hand over the doll's face, held the knife to the scalp, and pulled the hair across the blade. The strands came away in his hand reluctantly, like pulling a wing off a bird.

He rotated the defiled doll before his eyes and felt the excitement rise in his neck. Pretty little thing.

Dwayne dropped the doll to the carpet and stepped into Camille's bedroom. The kindergartner lay sideways on her Powerpuff Girls sheets, blond hair arrayed over the pillow like a yellow skirt.

Pretty little thing.

LORRAINE

Lorraine gazed at the martini just down the bar from where she sat. She shut her eyes, almost tasting it. Her own glass rattled when she lifted it to her lips, the ice betraying the tremors in her hand. Water. All it did was chill her. But at least it kept the gravel out of her voice.

"You really used to be a model?" the guy asked.

Lorraine forced herself to look at him. He was bulbous and sweaty, with meaty fingers like a stack of Michelin tires. The thought of him touching her ...

"Yeah," she said, "really. Magazines and catalogs and sh—" She censored herself. Maybe this guy was one of those pervs who didn't mind adultery but couldn't stand foul language. "Stuff."

His eyes widened and wandered somewhere south of her face. "That's really something, huh?"

"Yeah. So you sure you don't need the Percocet anymore?" He'd said it was his *wife's* painkiller, but there was no need to remind him that he was betraying her. It might blow the whole thing. Lorraine stamped down a shudder. She needed a smoke.

His eyes came back north. "Huh? Oh, right. No, no, she doesn't—I mean, it'll be fine."

Lorraine stood up and pressed herself against his shoulder. "I don't know about you, honey, but I'm ready to get somewhere private with you."

He almost fell getting off the barstool. "Yeah, sure. Definitely." He dropped a twenty on the bar and headed to the door, gripping her hand on his arm as if he thought she might run away.

She was going to run away, all right, but not just yet. She watched his jowls bounce as he walked and again thought of that face on hers.

"Just ... let's go grab the Percocet first, okay?"

"What? I can't go home with—"

She yanked her hand away and stopped. "You're going to get it first, you hear me. Or you don't get," she said, pulling the hem of her shirt wide open for him to have a look, "what you want."

His eyes bugged. "Right. Right. Okay. Come on."

She smoothed her shirt and preceded him to the door. Perv.

PROFANITY WITHOUT ALL THE BAD LANGUAGE

Were those characters foul? Were they profane? Did you *feel* their depravity in the seat of your being? If I did my job right, you were horrified by Dwayne and disgusted by Lorraine.

Surely these are the kind of people who would use profanity. Foulness pervaded their character. Even if you didn't actually see or hear them using four-letter words, you felt a deep corruption oozing through their skin.

Here's the point: It is quite possible to create the *feeling* of profanity without the *use* of profanity. In fact, doing so is superior to using profanity in your fiction. It's the better way, in my opinion.

In his novel *Rising Sun*, Michael Crichton creates a foul-mouthed detective character. He drops the F-bomb as commonly as the words *the* or *and*. He is truly the most disgusting, pathetic character I've ever seen on the pages of a novel.

This reaction may not have been what Crichton was aiming for. He probably wanted this character to seem intimidating and street-smart, but I just thought he was a sad and empty wretch, consumed by self-loathing.

In other words, the free and frequent use of profanity in a book does not necessarily create the hard-edged character you may be trying for. You may find the profanity working against you.

Conversely, the *absence* of profanity in a book does not mean you cannot create hard-edged or profane characters. As I hope I've demonstrated above.

SHOWING VS. TELLING

By this point in *The Art & Craft of Writing Christian Fiction*, you know how I feel about showing versus telling. If you've read any of my novels, you know how I feel about showing versus telling.

Anybody can write, "She was angry because of how he'd treated her on the plane." It takes a lot more skill from the writer to *communicate* that she was angry and that the cause of her anger was how he'd treated her on the plane—and to do so without saying it outright.

Telling is cheating, in my opinion. It's lazy storytelling. It reveals a low view of the reader's intelligence and a lack of trust in the author's own ability to convey information on paper. It stops the story cold and removes all mystery and bores the reader. It is, in short, a bad idea.

Showing, on the other hand, is the land where the masters dwell.

When it comes to communicating that a character is lost or profane, the frequent use of profanity in the manuscript is telling. It's lazy. Anyone can do it. Yep, that's a foul-mouthed person.

It takes more creativity and skill—not to mention more words—to *communicate* the character is lost or profane but to do so without the use of profanity itself. In other words, it's showing.

Which is more effective: Crichton's detective or Dwayne and Lorraine? Which method most perfectly conveys the dissoluteness of the character? Which method more insidiously reveals the person's degraded inner state? Which method better *shows* profanity?

Telling conveys head knowledge to the reader, and only faintly at that. Showing conveys heart knowledge. When you show something to your reader, she feels it at the center of her being. It enters her mind deeply. She remembers it well. That's what you want to accomplish when you have a foul character. You want your reader to feel it in her toes.

The next time you bring a debauched character onstage in your fiction, I challenge you to consider how you can reveal the character's foulness through scene, action, and thought instead of the direct use of profanity.

You may still use one or more of the solutions in the previous chapter. But always, *always* concentrate your efforts on how you can show your character being profane instead of just letting the epithets flow.

WINDING DOWN

We have reached the end of our last "Focus on the Craft" section. We have now covered almost everything I teach when it comes to writing Christian fiction.

As we near the conclusion of our time together in this book, it is fitting to think a minute about how to end your novel. We've already talked about being sure your ending arises from your beginning. Now let's talk about tying the ending into the beginning. It's called *circularity.*

chapter 52

CIRCULARITY

Early in my writing career I discovered something that lends an ineffable sense of completeness and poetic unity to my writing.

I was reading a book on brainstorming and netting out an idea using these charts where you start by writing a central thought on a page and then "web" out spin-off ideas from there. I don't remember what the book was called, but I remember the term I learned: *circularity.*

The author was saying you should create a short story or essay from the web you come up with on the page. The key component of the story's construction, the author said, was to begin the story with the central idea (that first circle in the middle of the page), and then at the conclusion of the story, refer back to it.

So let's say your central idea was *guitar.* That's what you wrote down first. You have some idea you know is floating around in your mind, but you haven't been able to pull it down to look at it clearly yet. But it has something to do with guitars. So you start spinning off thoughts from that idea.

In the course of your webbing you come to realize your elusive idea is really that Simon and Garfunkel had a huge influence on modern pop music.

Now that you've arrived at your real thought, it's time to write your essay. Your writing piece should begin with a discussion of a guitar (because that's where your own thinking began) and then it should move on to what the idea is mainly about. But when you're wrapping up your essay, make sure to come back to your image of the guitar.

Begin and end at essentially the same place. Come full circle. Circularity.

WANT WHOLE GRAINS WITH THAT?

Circularity imbues your fiction with this wonderful, holistic, Zen-like sense of completeness.

I have found it to be a remarkable tool in fiction. Used correctly, circularity gives your writing a lyrical feeling and implies to the reader that you knew at the beginning precisely where all this was going to go. (As if any novelist ever knows that!) Circularity makes your writing feel intentional and nicely wrapped up at the end.

You can use circularity in an entire book, in a single scene, or even with characters and themes.

How about some examples?

As I introduced in Chapter 22, I began my fourth novel, *Operation: Firebrand*, with this line: "Today I'm going to kill a man in cold blood."

You want to know who this person is. You think he's a serial killer or something. So you keep reading.

In that opening scene you learn that this character is a Navy SEAL deployed with his platoon in Indonesia and that he is the team's sniper. Now you start understanding why he could be about to kill a man in cold blood. *Ah,* you think, *he's a trained assassin. Interesting.*

But then you begin to read that he's uncomfortable with this situation, that he's undergone a change in his life, and he's no longer convinced that he should be doing this job. Uh, oh. Internal conflict. Even more interesting.

When it came time to end the scene, I decided to employ circularity. The last line of the scene is an almost exact repeat of the first line in the scene. Only when he says it this time, we know more about him and what he means. At the end, you realize it's not the mantra of a killer, but a cry for help: "Oh, Lord Jesus, today I am going to kill a man in cold blood."

Suddenly, with that last line, the scene is tied together like a ribbon around a present. You realize that the author knew what he was doing when he began this scene. It was like it had been all planned out. The reader begins to trust the author. The reader begins to love the book.

CIRCLE BACK AROUND

I don't know what it is about referring to the beginning at the end that makes a piece of writing feel complete, like a solid, intentional unit, but I'm telling you, it does.

Try it in your own writing. Write a short story or article and be conscious about constructing your beginning in a distinctive way and make sure your ending refers back to it. Maybe write the story two ways, once with no attempt at circularity and once with it. Let someone else read both and tell you which one is better.

I think circularity works best in smaller units, like a prologue or essay, as the beginning is still in the reader's mind after only a few pages. But if the beginning of your entire book is distinctive enough that the reader will remember it even at the end, four hundred pages later, then by all means use circularity and refer back to it.

I end this same novel, *Operation: Firebrand*, with a reference back to the beginning: "It wasn't what he'd expected all those mornings ago when he'd walked out to kill a man in cold blood. It was a lot better."

Whether the segment you're writing now is large or small, think about how you could add a nice dose of circularity. See if you can find a way at the end to refer back to the beginning. Use it within scenes, and use it with the book as a whole.

Your story unit will feel whole and finished, and your readers will acknowledge your all-around skills. Circularity is your friend.

chapter 53
LITERARY AGENTS

Way back in the Dark Ages when I was first writing for Christian publishers (circa 1994), a veteran acquisitions editor told me, "I'll never work with agents."

Three years later, you couldn't get a proposal looked at by that same editor, or by any Christian publishing company, without an agent.

The situation changed for everybody.

Twenty-plus years later, the situation is changing again.

A QUICK HISTORY

Thanks largely to the success of books like the Left Behind series, everyone figured out that there might be a future in Christian fiction. Suddenly publishers that hadn't published fiction started looking for novels, and just as suddenly, aspiring Christian novelists began coming out of the woodwork.

Whereas in years prior, acquisitions editors at Christian houses might have seen a couple hundred fiction proposals in a year, now they were seeing a thousand or more. Sadly, the vast majority wasn't worth being published.

The editor's available time to read all of these new proposals didn't magically increase with the workload. So what's a body to do? Some publishers opted to hire more editors to handle the increased volume, even having someone on staff whose only job was to read through the "slush pile" and identify those few worth looking at. But most did not. Either way, it didn't take long for publishers to realize that they shouldn't be spending so many manhours on something that yielded so little fruit.

It occurred to someone, or perhaps to the entire industry at once, that they could get the same results in a different way if only they had someone else do all the preliminary reading first. If this hypothetical *someone else* would read everything that came over the transom and weed out all but the very best, it would be a beautiful thing.

And thus the need for literary agents in the Christian publishing marketplace was born.

In a very short span, all the major Christian publishing houses declared themselves closed to "unsolicited manuscripts," which meant authors couldn't directly send them a proposal or a manuscript—it all had to come to them via an agent.

WHAT ARE AGENTS GOOD FOR, ANYWAY?

Sometimes Christian authors get frustrated about their inability to land an agent, so they decide maybe they don't need one. Indie authors almost certainly don't need an agent if all they're going to do is publish independently. So who should even try to get an agent, and why?

The situation I described above remains in effect today. The only way "in" at most traditional Christian publishing houses is with an agent. (Well, or if you know someone who works at the publishing house, or, and take note of this one, if you meet an editor at a Christian writers' conference.)

Actually, there are at least four great reasons for having an agent if you're hoping to be published traditionally (i.e., you're not going solely indie).

1. AGENTS GET YOUR BOOK LOOKED AT

As I've already outlined, most traditional Christian publishing houses won't even consider your novel unless it comes to them through an agent. This isn't snobbery on their part (usually); it's simple survival.

But what if you already have an in at one of these houses? What if you're related to the publisher or you have a published author friend who introduces you to her editor? What if you've gone to a Christian writers' conference and met the editor yourself, and she's asked you to send in your manuscript? Do you still need an agent if their main job—getting your book in front of the eyes of editors at a publishing house—has already been taken care of?

Well, it's up to you. But I still say yes. Because of reasons two through four.

2. AGENTS ARE INDUSTRY VETERANS

For the most part, literary agents serving the Christian publishing marketplace know that industry well. Many have been working in the business for a decade or more. Most have worked at publishing companies themselves. They know how the game is played. For an industry outsider, that's an invaluable ally to have.

It's especially true now that many agents are industry veterans because so many publishing companies are shedding editors and other longtimers like crazy, and many of them—far too many, in my opinion—are becoming agents. But we'll look at that in a minute.

It's never a bad thing to have an experienced industry pro on your side. Some agents will even serve as career counselors, too, giving sound counsel on what the author should do or how to interpret various options.

3. AGENTS SPEAK CONTRACTESE

Agents speak the language of publishers. One day, God willing, you are going to have a publisher willing to go to contract on something you've written. They'll send you the standard agreement (not the standard rich-and-famous contract, by the way), and you'll look at it. Then you'll look at it some more. Then you'll wonder why, when you're a reasonably intelligent adult, you can't make heads or tails of it. You'll go to the dictionary and look up *turpitude*. And then you'll wish you had someone on your team who could explain what in the world you're looking at.

Enter the agent. A good literary agent speaks legalese, at least that dialect of it that pertains to publishing agreements. An agent will open it up and say, "Okay, skip all this page … blah-blah-blah … Hmm, that's interesting … Ah, we'll want to change that … ." and so forth. In other words, it will make perfect sense to an agent. And, importantly, the agent will know which things are negotiable and which things aren't.

Nothing gives a publishing company heartburn more than having to work with a new author who is convinced the publisher is trying to rip her off and who hires the family lawyer to "suggest some revisions."

Granted, the publishing contract is geared to favor the publishing company. But after all, who is taking the risk here? Who is shelling out the money to publish your book? If it feels like a financing contract at Jim's Used Car Palace, you're not far off. But that doesn't mean you're being ripped off (well, maybe you are at Jim's).

I've seen publishers get so frustrated over authors and lawyers who questioned standard contract boilerplate that they were willing to cancel the contract rather than keep working with such a problematic author. Not a great way to begin your relationship with that publishing house.

And it all could've been avoided if only you'd had an agent.

4. AGENTS MEDIATE DISPUTES

I know it will shock you to learn this, but sometimes Christians have disagreements. Arguments, even. Christian publishing is not immune from such things, I assure you. Sometimes things get so heated—or are so delicate—between an author and a publisher that somebody else better step in, and fast.

Let's say you feel that the publisher promised X but didn't deliver. You remember them saying something about the cover design or something about the marketing or something about changing the release date, but you don't see it happening. You could call up your editor and let her have it with both barrels, but that's not likely to help anyone. Or, if you have an agent, you could just have that person make the call. He or she will be glad to do so, but not without first saying, "You should've gotten it in writing!"

Agents also help the *publisher* when disputes arise. If the author is not performing as promised (a situation that is, sadly, much more common than the publisher being at fault), the agent—not the author—gets the call from the publishing-house representative. It's nice for the publisher to have someone to call who understands the business well enough to see that the author is behaving incorrectly and can then translate that into language the author can understand without the editor having to be the bad guy.

If you're self-publishing, and that's all you aspire to do for now, you don't need a literary agent. If you've published so many books that you understand publishing, can read contracts, and have plenty of contacts in the industry, you also may not need an agent. But if you want to be published by a traditional Christian house, and you're nearer the front end of your career than the back end, I recommend trying to land an agent.

HOW DO YOU GET AN AGENT?

Okay, so I've convinced you that having an agent is a good thing, yes? I hope so. And now you'd like to know how to get one a' them-thar agents fer yerself.

If you happen to be attending one of the major Christian writers' conferences, you're in luck: Several of the top agents will probably be in attendance. Schedule yourself an appointment with each one of them, talk with them about your book(s), and get a feel for whether you think your personalities would be a good fit.

If you think so, and the agent thinks so, he will probably ask you to submit the full manuscript for consideration. If he likes it, he'll send you an agreement form, and you guys will hopefully agree to work together. That agreement will remain in effect until one or both of you decides to dissolve the relationship and move on. (It's not a marriage; it's a business relationship. If things don't work out between you as you'd hoped, break it off and find someone else. The agent may do the same to you.)

If you're not planning on going to one of those Christian writers' conferences … well, then, change your plans. Why wouldn't you go? Consider it an investment and an education. Plus, you'll get great support from folks more or less like you.

If you can't get to a conference, and you just have no clue who to even try to get as your agent, grab the latest edition of *The Christian Writer's Market Guide* and peruse the section on agents who serve the Christian market.

Another strategy is to check the copyright page of Christian novels you love. Many times the agent's name will be listed there, giving you the ability to find out a few agents who have represented authors who may be similar to you.

When you're ready to contact an agent you've identified, you'll need to pitch your book to that person just the way you would've pitched it to a publishing company in years past: engaging query letter, great proposal with sample chapters, and the full manuscript standing by and available upon request.

There's still a slush pile, Dorothy. It's just been moved to agents' in-boxes.

CAVEAT EMPTOR

A few safety tips before I send you off on the Great Agent Chase.

First, agents take a cut of what you earn from your writing, usually 15 percent. That's how they make their living. If you were to get a check for $1,000 from a publishing company, that would be $850 to you and $150 to your agent. That holds true for advances, royalty checks, and anything else pertaining to a project the agent placed at a publisher for you.

Don't begrudge an agent her 15 percent, by the way. Without her, you probably wouldn't be getting your 85 percent in the first place.

Second, agents get paid only when you do. In other words, when you get paid for your writing, the agent gets paid. And not before.

If you're in talks with an "agent" who wants to charge you anything up front—reading fees, copying fees, handling fees, etc.—run screaming away. That person is a scam artist trying to rip you off.

An agent gets paid by placing his clients' writing projects at publishing companies. When the publisher pays the author, that's when the agent gets paid.

SO MANY AGENTS

The third caveat, as I write this, is that there are currently too many agents serving the Christian publishing industry, in my opinion. Christian houses are in financial trouble. Many are folding or combining with others or are being bought up. Most are hanging on by a thread, hoping for a few blockbusters to keep them going for another six months.

Because of this, many houses are trimming their staffs. Some of the Christian publishing professionals getting the ax are editors who have been playing this game for years. The dump of publishing veterans into the ranks of the unemployed has resulted in many of them deciding to become agents.

It makes sense from a certain point of view (thank you, Obi Wan). These former editors have had years of friendly dealings with agents, so they know plenty of places where they might fit. These former editors know how publishing works, and some can even speak contractese.

The problem with this is that we are in a publishing climate that has turned cold. Publishing companies have less money to offer for new books and fewer publishing slots to fill. Midlist novelists have been cut loose from their contracts, resulting in much more competition for those few remaining slots.

And into this environment of lack comes a new army of agents. So you have more and more agents fighting for fewer and fewer publishing opportunities.

If you're suddenly getting images of a feeding frenzy, you're thinking the right way.

The old publishing model is on life support. It may hang on for a while, and it might even be able to gain new life somehow. But at the moment it appears that the industry is top-heavy and bloated with agents fighting for less and less money and fewer and fewer publishing slots.

Many agents have seen the handwriting on the wall and are trying to adapt. Some have begun offering publishing services to help their clients self-publish. Some have started their own imprints. At least one I know of has purchased a small publishing company himself and will run it alongside his agenting business. I foresee a great falling away of agents as they come to realize there's just not enough "food" to feed them all.

If you are hoping to get published in the traditional Christian publishing industry, you need an agent, even after everything I've just said. Be sure you're going with someone who has a good track record, can and will supply references, and is making sales now with major Christian publishers.

chapter 54
SEEKING PUBLICATION

Many people want to write a novel someday, but most of those who actually accomplish that feat are interested in more than just the accomplishment.

They'd really like to see their book on the shelf.

So anyone can read it. Even Aunt Betty, who said you'd never amount to much. Even your kids. Even your boss. Even people you've never heard of. *Especially* people you've never heard of.

As long as you've gone to all the work to write this thing, why not see if you can get it in print?

Let's explore how you might go about that.

THE PHASES OF "READY"

Some novelists are so eager to get published that they rush their rough draft right out to agents, editors, and friends of cousins whose neighbor's cat's veterinarian knows a guy who used to be in publishing.

I used to get this sort of e-mail on a regular basis. It has an undisclosed recipient list, begins with "To Whom It May Concern," and proceeds to gush about the sender's awesome manuscript, which is certain to be a bestseller, revolutionize publishing, and reinstate Pluto as a planet (Go, Team Pluto!).

The sender has obviously sent out a mass e-mail to everyone he could find. He certainly hasn't bothered to research any of the publishers he's contacting—obvious because the book he's pushing is a nonfiction book about snails, and I published only speculative fiction with a supernatural edge.

In his eagerness to reach out to anyone who might possibly be interested, the only thing he has hastened to do is get his e-mail deleted. And, if the publisher has a good memory, to get himself put on a blacklist forever.

I don't know what helped you slog through the long, hard work of writing a novel. Possibly it was the thought of publication that kept you going. If that's true, even in part, I would urge you to apply the brakes and shift into park for a while.

If your book is amazing, it will get published. In truth, anything can get published, especially in today's publishing environment, and this will certainly be true of books of a higher quality. So there's no rush. It's not like today is the last day publishers will ever want to look at unpublished fiction, so you'd better hurry! We passed Y2K and the Mayan Doomsday pretty well, so until the End Times begin, fiction publishers will continue to need fiction manuscripts.

It's also not as though publishers have a dearth of excellent manuscripts to evaluate, so you'd better get yours in today. Nor is it (probably) the case that your idea is so breathtakingly original that your book will be fabulously published even if it's not really ready, and you'd better copyright and trademark and bronze-plate it so everyone will know it's yours, your own ... your *Precious*.

Let's just wait a bit, all right? It's much better to go slow, do your research, polish your novel, learn the biz, survey the landscape, and then send it off intelligently than it is to rush it out the door and think you can just sit back and wait for the fat royalty checks to start rolling in.

There are phases of readiness that every fiction manuscript, and every novelist, goes through. Or, rather, that every manuscript and novelist *should* go through. Today, it's possible for a book to be published long before it's actually ready, and that doesn't do anyone any favors, especially the author.

Here's the path an unpublished manuscript often takes:

1. The author writes the novel.
2. The author sends it (the full manuscript or just a proposal or query) to agents and publishers.
3. The manuscript is rejected by everyone and his parrot.
4. The author feels she wasn't cut out to be a novelist after all.
5. The author gets mad/gets a second wind and starts trying to figure out why the book was so soundly rejected.
6. The author learns to improve her fiction skills.
7. The author learns the publishing landscape.

8. The author meets lots of people in the industry.
9. The author learns a better approach for sending out her much improved manuscript and a better person or set of people to send it to.
10. The author sends it out a second time (hoping no one remembers her first attempt) and either gets published or at least gets much closer to that goal.

Here's the path I'm urging you to take:

1. You write your novel.
2. You resist the urge to send it to everyone and his parrot.
3. You go through this book and other teaching/critiquing aids to improve it to the highest level you're able to take it.
4. You survey the publishing landscape and meet people in the industry.
5. You research your publishing options.
6. You start working on your marketing plan and platform.
7. You decide whether you want to attempt to procure a literary agent.
8. You shop the book around in an intelligent manner and take charge of your publishing career.

Sound better? Let's talk about this path one step at a time.

IMPROVING YOUR NOVEL

You've already jogged down this particular road a fair distance, simply by applying the things you've learned in this book. But there are always more books and articles to read!

Book learning is great, if you're someone who can learn from a book. I am that kind of person, and because you're reading this, I can assume you are. But other people learn in other ways. That's neither good nor bad but simply how things are.

Your goal is to get your manuscript to the highest level of quality you can achieve. We know that the end user may not care about quality, but you should. Agents and editors certainly do (most say they do, at least). I'm hoping you'll take it upon yourself to learn the skills and techniques of excellent fiction, rather than simply paying someone else to take it beyond your level of capability or interest. I suspect you want to bring these skills onboard yourself, or, again, you wouldn't have bothered to make it so far in this book.

So here are the tools and services that can elevate your novel and your fiction craftsmanship. Most serious writers will eventually use all the items on the list.

- **Write:** Simply writing lots of fiction will improve your writing on some levels. Certain things—not least the mastery of your word-processing program—will become second nature for you if you do. Of course, if you're starting with bad habits, writing more and more might just solidify them; best to keep moving down this list.
- **Read Good Fiction:** Few things inspire you to perform at your utmost potential more than examples you admire.
- **Read Books and Articles on Craft:** If you're a book learner, by all means avail yourself of the many books on the craft of fiction writing. *Writer's Digest* has a wonderful selection of winners, as do other publishers. But book learning may not be your style, and in any case a book can take you only so far; sometimes it's very difficult to take what the book advocates and discern whether you're doing it or not doing it in your own writing. That's where objective eyes help.
- **Use Critique Partners:** If you don't have a crit partner yet or aren't already a member of a (healthy) critique group, consider doing something about that posthaste. A good crit partner/group can be hugely valuable not only in helping you see what has become invisible to you and in giving you constructive feedback about how to improve your manuscript, but also in giving you access to people who have perhaps been studying publishing longer than you have and may be able to help you understand what's going on in that world.
- **Go to Writers' Conferences:** Unless you live far out in the sticks, the chances are good that there is an annual Christian writers' conference within driving distance of your home, and many across the United States are worth flying out to. The three

great things about writers' conferences are (1) you meet other crazy novelists like yourself (including folks who might be future critique partners for you), (2) you get advice about craft and the industry from experts in the field (the larger conferences are more likely to have a world-class faculty than the locals, but sometimes the little ones can surprise you), and (3) you get direct access to literary agents and editors from Christian publishing houses and can pitch your manuscript directly to them. The latter reason is the best benefit for going to these events. How better to learn the industry and get "in" with pros than to meet them face to face? Invest in yourself and go to a writers' conference this year.

- **Join an Online Fiction Training Service:** A phenomenon of the twenty-first century is the rise of online training services for pretty much anything you want to get trained in. I operate FictionAcademy.com, which contains streaming video of all my teaching. There are several services like this popping up all the time now. Nothing like having the writers'-conference experience without shelling out hundreds or thousands of dollars, having to leave home, clearing your schedule, or even taking off your fuzzy slippers. The other benefit of these is that, if you can find one with a good teacher, your level of instruction will be consistently high (while the quality of teaching you get at writers' conferences is hit or miss), plus you can watch the videos over and over rather than having to rely on the notes you took when you heard it live.
- **Hire a Freelance Editor:** This one will require us to break out of our lovely bulleted list and go back to paragraph form. Read on.

WORKING WITH A FREELANCE EDITOR

In my mind, there is nothing more valuable you can do to improve your novel—and your own writing skill—than to work with a freelance editor. Editors are, after all, professionals at taking a promising manuscript and turning it into the sort of excellence we expect from major publishing houses. They can take a C+ manuscript and turn it into an A manuscript. And because most of the aforementioned major publishing houses have fired their editors and dumped them onto the freelance market (where most of them have become agents!), you have access to virtuosos you'd otherwise not be able to so much as meet unless you were under contract at that house.

The problem is that there are also exactly one bajillion lousy freelance editors out there, and you probably have no way of knowing which is which.

You can't rely on the fact that someone calls herself a professional editor, because you could call yourself that. Anyone could make such a claim. You could even have business cards printed up saying so, whether it's true or not. You can't rely on the fact that the person previously worked as an editor at a publishing house, because some publishing houses employ lousy editors.

Even if you find a bona fide professional editor who has experience with fiction, you can't know that she's any good. Perhaps everything she'll say about your manuscript is exactly wrong—or wrong for you. How would you know? Well, you might have a little knowledge of what's what if you've done the other items on the bulleted list you just read, but even writers of fiction how-to books and articles don't agree with one another.

It's enough to boggle the mind and tempt you to skip this phase altogether. But I urge you to persist. If you can find an editor who is truly helpful, you will have found a gold mine. Nothing in publishing is more beneficial to you and your career than a terrific fiction editor.

FINDING A GREAT FREELANCE EDITOR

First, ask around. Have your writing friends worked with a freelancer they found especially helpful? Why not start there?

Second, do your homework. When you get a name, check out the person's webpage, blog, or Facebook presence. See if you connect with his personality and style as expressed there. See also if you can find his rates.

Most people new to writing get sticker shock when they learn how much freelance editors cost. Of course you can pay much less and much more, but to receive a full enchilada edit on a 100,000-word manuscript, you can expect to pay $2,500 to $5,000. And upwards of $8,000 to $12,000 or more for the award winners and very best editors in the industry. You can pay less than this, but sometimes you get what you pay for. Other times, you pay a lot and *don't* get what you pay for. Which brings us back to our question of how not to get burned.

Check Preditors & Editors (pred-ed.com) for that person's name. The site lists people who have been identified as scam artists. One important caveat to this is that some people are unfairly placed on that list, so don't take it as gospel. But if you find that person's name on the preditors side, apply some extra caution. Ask the editor for references and then actually communicate with the references.

In the end, there's no better way to find out if an editor is going to be a good fit for you than to have her edit your fiction. Some editors will do sample edits for you (two to ten double-spaced pages is common) for free. Others will charge you a small fee to do so. Find out how much it would cost for that person to do a full edit on the opening ten to twenty pages of your manuscript. Chances are it would be a lot more affordable to do this—between fifty and two hundred dollars, probably—than to go for the full edit without first taking this step.

Then, if you like what the person did on the sample edit, and if you believe it will truly improve your book and your writing, go for it. Maybe take the plunge and pay for the full edit or have her do another segment of your book. You're the boss here, so you can work within your budget. At worst, if you don't like what the editor has done, or maybe she did almost nothing to the pages but happily took your two Benjamins, you can just keep looking for the right editor.

Editors have been known to take novels that would otherwise quickly fall upon the literary trash heap and turn them into award winners and/or bestsellers.

I can't tell you how many novelists have come to me, in my role as freelance editor and book doctor, wondering what in the world is going on with all these rejections. They've struck out, and they want to know why. Abandoning their notion that they could just write it, send it out, and get famous, they're finally willing to get serious about improving it.

That's another thing you want to look for in an editor: Can he diagnose what's working and what's not working in your manuscript? Perhaps instead of paying two hundred dollars to have him do a trial edit, instead pay whatever he charges to simply read through the whole manuscript and give you a brief write-up of what he sees as the strengths, weaknesses, and the way forward for your book (this is sometimes called an editorial review).

Also remember that many authors work as freelance editors on the side. Be sure to scour author websites (like www.jeffgerke.com) to see what kind of editorial services they may offer.

UNDERSTANDING PUBLISHING TODAY

Getting your novel up to snuff may take you a while—up to a year or even longer. Don't be in a hurry. Before the aforementioned End Times, publishers will continue to need new fiction manuscripts to publish.

The next two items on our big bulleted list above are to survey the publishing landscape and meet people in the industry and to research your publishing options. I'll address those together.

First, let's talk about understanding the publishing landscape, by which I mean exploring whether you're hoping to be traditionally published, to self-publish, or to try a new publishing option.

GOING TRADITIONAL OR NONTRADITIONAL

In general, it is more blessed to be paid than to pay. When it comes to having your novel published, it's always ideal to have someone other than you shell out the cash for bringing it to market. Thus the traditional publishing avenue is the one most people prefer to take.

In that scenario, the writer receives an advance (some amount of money, usually between $1,500 and $6,000 for first-time novelists), takes the manuscript through a professional edit, receives a professionally produced cover, and sees his novel released nationally in bookstores and online. If the book ever breaks even ("earns out"), the author will begin receiving royalty payments periodically.

For generations, this has been the primary publishing model in America. It's still what people think of when they think of getting published. Their imaginings also usually include multicity book tours, champagne parties in Manhattan, and movies based on the book.

As you might guess, this didn't happen very often, even in the heyday of publishing.

We are no longer in said heyday. The downturn in the economy, the rise of electronic publishing, and a shift in the mood of the day has brought about the slow collapse of that model. It will hang around for a while in much smaller form, but for the most part, the Golden Age is gone.

Novelist Athol Dickson sums it up nicely:

> "Authors no longer need traditional publishers (or their contracts) for editing, cover design, interior design, bulk printing discounts, warehousing, distribution, marketing, promotion, or sales. The only thing left is management (i.e., oversight of the above so the author doesn't have to think about it) and the advance, which means the industry has been reduced to offering nothing authors can't do themselves except for providing venture capital.
>
> I can't think of any other industry that survived after becoming irrelevant in nine out of ten of the key services it offered—unless the players made massive structural changes to their way of doing business, and we've seen none of that."

In the place of the traditional publishing model has come a panoply of new publishing opportunities. Small presses, niche presses, print on demand (POD), e-publishing, app publishing, transmedia, and, of course, self-publishing have exploded onto the scene, and we find ourselves hip deep in a publishing revolution.

Many authors—primarily those who were living large under the old publishing model—have bemoaned these changes. Large traditional Christian publishers are folding or being purchased and combined. Bookstores are closing in droves. Consequently, the remaining traditional publishers are being even more conservative than they were before. Advances are smaller, they're taking fewer chances on new authors, and beloved midlist authors—many of the names you know—are finding themselves without new contracts. Publishers compete for the few surefire home-run hitters, and everyone else is left in the dugout.

So it's no wonder authors are complaining about these changes. But I have maintained for years that there's never been a better time to be a writer than now. Never, as in ever. As in since the dawn of mankind.

Until today, restrictions on how easily a writer could reach a reader with her message existed. Before Gutenberg, the restriction was that only the clergy and a few others even knew how to read or write or had access to mass production of printed material. Then you had to have great wealth to use that movable type press and get the books out to people far and wide. Across the centuries, it has been the large publishers who put up the money for books to be made and distributed, and so they were the ones who controlled what got published and what did not. And what got published was what would sell enough units to pay off the large cost of producing and distributing the book.

Nowhere in there did the small-time author sitting at his desk have the ability to get his book broadcast to the world. Sure, we've had self-publishing for a while, but it was exceedingly rare for a self-published book to reach a wide readership. Most such books ended up in boxes gathering dust in the (poorer) author's garage. And, yes, we've had the Internet for a while, but so long as the old publishing model was going strong and e-readers were rare, most electronically published books never reached a wide readership, despite the technical possibility for it to happen.

But now, today, for free, you could upload your manuscript to Amazon, and people across the globe could be reading it on their devices in minutes. You could begin collecting money from your writing before you went to bed tonight.

Hang on a second though! There are a billion reasons why you might not want to do that and why you probably wouldn't make much money. Still, the point remains that you *could*. You have at your disposal the potential to reach tens of millions of readers without any up-front cost to you and without any middleman (other than Amazon or whoever).

It's a great day, especially for the previously marginalized sort of book and the previously marginalized sort of author. Before, if you weren't writing what was perceived to be "hot," you couldn't get published at all. Those lightly esteemed off-genres like true crime or Western or military or Christian fantasy/SF were simply out of the question.

Now it's possible to get *your* novel to *exactly* the readership who wants *exactly* what you like to write.

There's never been a time like this in history, and I hope you take advantage of it.

The question for you, then, becomes whether you want to pursue traditional or nontraditional publishing.

My counsel is to try to get paid before deciding you're going to pay. Unless you know without a doubt that your book will simply never, ever find a publisher who wants to take it on (and pay you for it), I recommend giving that option a try.

Here's the hierarchy you might consider:

- Target a large traditional publisher who will pay you an advance, give your book a full edit and a good cover and marketing support, and all the trimmings.
- Target a midsized traditional publisher who will pay you an advance and do as many of the other things as possible.
- Target a small traditional publisher who will pay you an advance and do as many of the other things as possible.
- Target a niche publisher who will either pay you an advance or at least not charge you anything. Hopefully they will give you a decent edit and cover and other stuff but very little marketing, probably.
- Target a custom publishing company that will allow you to self-publish for free or very little expense (research CreateSpace and Lulu, for starters).
- Cobble together your own publishing team (editor, cover designer, copy editor, typesetter, marketer, printer, and any others you need), each of whom you pay as freelancers; you bear the expenditures, but you retain complete control and can pull the plug whenever you wish (so long as you pay what you owe, of course).
- E-publish only (hopefully after using a freelance editor and cover designer, at the least) and see if there is enough reader interest to go to a print version of the book through print on demand.
- Pay lots of money to a self-publishing company that offers a package you like and can afford.

Each of these options has advantages and disadvantages, and each one could be the right solution for you at different points in your publishing career.

If you go with self-publishing—either in print or electronic form, or both—understand that there is no guarantee you'll make back your money. In fact, you probably won't recoup your expenses (unless you go the free route). To have the best chance of recovering your money, you'll need to do lots of marketing, which we'll address later.

The myth being propagated out there today is that all you have to do is e-publish a book, and it will be hugely successful. But the "If you build it, they will come" approach is, indeed, a myth. Sure, the guys who already have big sales can put out a new e-book, and it will sell a million copies. But that same dynamic doesn't work for 99.99 percent of the rest of the authors putting out e-books.

Many authors turn to self-publishing ("custom publishing" or "independent publishing," it's called now) for strategic reasons. They're hoping to make such a big splash with their self-published book that it will attract the interest of those few remaining traditional publishers, who will come calling with a six- or seven-figure advance.

Or perhaps they are already published, but they are feeling stymied by their traditional publishing contracts. The going wisdom used to be that someone known for writing legal thrillers shouldn't start writing zombie books, but the author may frankly want to write zombie books—or zombie legal thrillers—so he does it on his own via custom publishing. And in some cases, it works fabulously.

The other great thing about indie publishing is that you keep most of the dough yourself. Yes, you have to pay out to get published, but all the profit comes to you. You'll have to give some to Amazon, but the lion's share of the profits finds its way to your *pocketses*. And if you do recoup your expenses, you have the chance for serious money.

The clout of traditional publishing houses is fading. Even if you do land a contract with one of them, it may not include an edit! You almost certainly won't get much marketing support. You could end up paying for those things out of your own pocket. And as for getting your book into bookstores, there are fewer and fewer of those establishments every day. Suddenly novelists are beginning to look around and say, "Wait, tell me again why I need a publishing house?" The answer is usually a silence punctuated only by chirping crickets.

Now, again, it's more blessed to be paid than to pay. But times have changed in publishing, and traditional publishing houses have gone from being the only legitimate game in town to being merely one of many alternatives.

EXPLORING THE PUBLISHING INDUSTRY

Simultaneous with your efforts to raise your manuscript to the highest level of fiction craftsmanship you can attain, you should begin working to learn the publishing industry.

The best ways to do that are to read industry magazines and blogs and go to writers' conferences.

The primary publishing-industry magazine is *Publishers Weekly*, which you can usually find in your library, or you can buy a subscription and read it online. *PW* has great book reviews and articles on trends, but it also covers news in the industry. It is the magazine that publishing professionals themselves read. Another good one is *Library Journal*.

With a little snooping around online, you can find blogs written by influential people in the publishing industry. Peruse a copy of *PW*, note the names of editors and agents being quoted, and then search for blogs by those people online. *Writer's Digest* magazine puts out an annual list of the best blogs on writing. Some terrific material awaits you.

Then consider writers' conferences again. If you attend three major Christian writers' conferences in the field of publishing that you hope to break into—and if you put yourself out there while you attend, actually introducing yourself to faculty, pitching your novel's idea to agents and editors, and having appointments with faculty in which you just ask for advice—you will quickly gain a working grasp of the publishing industry.

If you could attend all three conferences in a six-month period, you'd really have your finger on the pulse of it. Or, at least as much as someone on the periphery can have a finger on the pulse of any industry.

Plus, going to Christian writers' conferences allows you to become familiar with people who are in a position to help you get your book published through the traditional publishing route. After the conference, you can contact those people via e-mail, remind them about your great meeting at the conference, and ask if they'd like to see your latest manuscript or proposal. Agents and editors are more likely to respond to you well and in a timely manner if they've met you.

MARKETING

Right away, let me say that no one knows how to market fiction successfully. Oh, sure, if you're in charge of promoting the next J.K. Rowling book, and you have an unlimited budget, you can do it. But when it comes to an author whom most people haven't heard of—and when you're doing it on a limited budget—it's not so easy.

If there were a surefire way to successfully market a novel, everyone would be doing it, and every book so marketed would be a runaway bestseller. But such is not the case. No one knows.

However, it is possible to do a number of things that can give your novel a statistical chance at becoming a bestseller. Most of the time, those things don't work. But authors who do them are more likely to be successful (or less likely to be unsuccessful) than authors who don't.

This isn't a book on marketing, and I'm no expert on it. But I will say that marketing is all about letting people who would like your product know your product exists. All your marketing efforts, no matter how your book has gotten published, should be directed toward getting it in front of potential lovers of your book in a way that makes them want a copy for themselves.

I'll give you my 30:1 Rule of Marketing. For every thirty things you do to market your book, one of them will work. Unfortunately, you probably won't know which one of the thirty it was that worked, and even if you did know and you repeated it, it wouldn't work again. So you have to keep doing your thirties to get the ones.

But this rule works very nicely when applied to a monthly discipline. Every day, do one thing to market your book. Even if it's small, like sending an e-mail to a newspaper asking if they'd be willing to review your book. After roughly thirty days, you will have done roughly thirty things to promote your book … and one of them will have found traction. You will do this until you finally have enough ones piled atop one another that word of mouth takes over.

If you can get to that point—and most books never do—it will take on a life of its own. I wish you every success!

WHAT ABOUT BEFORE MY BOOK IS PUBLISHED?

In the meantime, even before your book is published, you can and should be working to build your so-called publishing platform.

Whole books have been written on the subject of *platform*. Essentially platform is how many people will automatically buy your book as soon as it's available.

A writer who is also a national media personality—with, say, a syndicated radio talk show—has a massive platform. As soon as a book by this person it available, even for preorder, millions of people will buy it.

Most of us have a less impressive platform. Most of us, if our first novel came out, could count on a whole five or six people buying it. A platform of that size is not going to impress any publishers. They, of course, prefer authors who have large built-in audiences.

What can you do to build your platform? Start doing things that will cause more people to become aware of you. Begin a blog that is not just about you and your writing journey but is about something that will appeal to the same reader who will love your novel when it comes out. Let people come to love your personality, and they'll be inclined to see about this book you've written. Try to get speaking gigs that pertain to your book topic and ask if you can sell books at a table in the back. Write magazine articles on topics that appeal to the same readership you'll be after for your novel.

If you're hoping to be traditionally published, you may not be able to build a platform large enough to impress them, not even if you worked on it for a year or more. But if you're in the market for a small press—and especially if you're self-publishing—you'll want as many people as possible to know about you before the book comes out.

Most Christian novelists I know absolutely hate the idea of marketing. Either they shy away from self-promotion on ethical grounds, or they're naturally mousy types who would rather write ten novels than market even one. If that's you, maybe save your energy from the blogging and speaking and instead save up money to hire a freelance publicity/marketing person (preferably one who rocks the social-media sites) to do it for you if and when your book is released.

But even the quivering mice among us can follow the 30:1 rule.

CONCLUSION

All right, my friend, we've come to the end of our time together. So I'd like to take a bit of my own advice and use some circularity here at the end. Here goes.

I love Christian fiction.

I love writing it. I love editing it. I love teaching it at writers' conferences. And I love publishing it through my small publishing house, Marcher Lord Press.

More, I love the people who write Christian fiction.

I hope *The Art & Craft of Writing Christian Fiction* has been helpful to you. Hopefully you've learned some things, gotten some issues straight, thought about some things in new ways, and maybe even had a chortle or two.

I loved writing the Fiction Writing Tip of the Week column. It was so great to be able to take the teaching I was delivering to individual writers and have a forum for helping any writers who happened to come by the page.

And it's been terrific fun having the chance to rework the material for book form. The "Focus on the Craft" sections were especially gratifying. Each one could be a daylong seminar, and put together it's at least a weeklong continuing track of fiction instruction like you'd get at a conference. I hope you've felt you've gotten your money's worth.

I actually have much more to teach. For this book, I've restricted this volume to what you need to know as you approach the writing of your novel and what you need to know to write the novel.

Writing fiction is pretty much the coolest job in the world. And writing *Christian* fiction takes a cool job and turns it into a ministry and a privilege. To serve God by imagining wonderful story people and telling amazing tales of adventure, woe, romance, and truth … I'm telling you, it doesn't get any better than that.

The Art & Craft of Writing Christian Fiction is my effort to both encourage and equip you to best serve your Lord by producing novels of excellence and mastery.

INDEX